# 1001
## GREATEST
## THINGS
## EVER SAID
## ABOUT
## CALIFORNIA

## ALSO FROM THE LYONS PRESS

# 1001
# GREATEST
# THINGS
# EVER SAID
# ABOUT
# CALIFORNIA

Edited and with an Introduction by
Steven D. Price

THE LYONS PRESS
Guilford, Connecticut
An imprint of The Globe Pequot Press

# Contents

California is the only state in the union where you can fall asleep under a rose bush in full bloom and freeze to death.

—W. C. Fields

# INTRODUCTION

Four blind men encounter an elephant. One touches a leg and concludes the animal is like a tree trunk. One holds the tail and calls it a whip. Another touches the elephant's trunk and decides the animal is like a hose. The fourth man feels the animal's side and calls it a wall.

A wise man who was watching told them, "All of you are right."

California, someone once reflected, is similar to the elephant in that parable. Visit Los Angeles, and you might well come away with the idea that all Californians are image-conscious people who have forgotten how to walk. See San Francisco, and you'd conclude that the entire state is populated with avant-garde free thinkers. Visit Orange County, and you'd say that conservatives hold sway. Equally varied is the state's terrain, ranging from the rugged northern coast to lush beaches in the south, from Sierra Nevada's majestic peaks to Death Valley's blistering, arid depths.

Not only does California have something for everyone, it knows what it has, and it's more than willing to share with the rest of the country. "Whatever starts in California unfortunately has a tendency to spread," President Jimmy Carter reportedly remarked during a 1977 cabinet meeting. For better or worse, California has indeed been the genesis of trends, including popular music (from the Beach Boys to the Grateful Dead), food ("health foods" and sushi), entertainers turned politicians (Ronald Reagan, Sonny Bono, and Arnold Schwarzenegger), and—fer shur—language (surfer- and Valley Girl–speak).

As you read through this celebration of the state's multifaceted and often contradictory personality, certain themes recur. One is golden, literally and figuratively. From the Forty-Niners' mining of the precious mineral to the bronzed beach boys and girls, the Gate has always been Golden. The state clearly has its adherents, and their words of praise are contained throughout, starting with the overview in the first chapter. However, the esteem in which the rest of the world—and indeed some Californians—holds the state is not uniformly high. Truman Capote once sneered, "It's a scientific fact that if you stay in California you lose one point of your IQ every year." Saul Bellow chose a particularly trenchant simile: "California is like an artificial limb the rest of the country doesn't really need." And there's Fred Allen's oft-quoted, "California's a wonderful place to live—if you happen to be an orange."

The book then goes on to present a panorama of the state's history, from the earliest Spanish settlers through Sutter's Mill and the increased population thereafter to the horrors of San Francisco's 1906 earthquake to the heyday of Haight-Ashbury in the Sixties and Silicon Valley's latter-day gold rush.

John Steinbeck, Robert Louis Stevenson, and Joaquin Miller are among the authors and poets whose works in "The Treasure Veins: California in Literature" offer insights and praise (other slices of fiction and nonfiction from the likes of novelist and essayist Joan Didion, mystery writer Dashiell Hammett, and *auteur*/author Woody Allen will be found sprinkled throughout).

Think of California and two cities spring to mind, and both deserve entire chapters. Los Angeles is one: "Los Angeles is seventy-two suburbs in search of a city," Dorothy Parker quipped, while Robert Redford predicted that "If you stay in Beverly Hills too long, you become a Mercedes."

If much of what is said about L.A. are put-downs, San Francisco elicits celebrations. Case in point: Norman Mailer's "Los Angeles is a constellation of plastic; San Francisco is a lady." Dylan Thomas raved, "You wouldn't think such a place as San Francisco could exist. The wonderful sunlight there, the hills, the great bridges, the Pacific at your shoes."

Of course, we must not forget that there's more to California than La-La-Land and the City by the Bay, which is presented in "The Chosen Spots." A number of people quoted here are not usually associated with their subjects, such as Thomas Mann on Santa Monica ("The light, the dry, always refreshing warmth; the spaciousness, the ocean . . .") and Simone de Beauvoir on Pasadena ("Suburbs, developments, and intersections . . . Softly sloping avenues loll between orange trees and thickset palms").

Although properly part of Los Angeles, no one would deny that Hollywood's a world unto itself, entitled to its own separate chapter. "Hollywood's a place where they'll pay you a thousand dollars for a kiss, and fifty cents for your soul. I know, because I turned down the first offer often enough and held out for the fifty cents," Marilyn Monroe lamented. Observed Groucho Marx, "Ever since they found out that Lassie was a boy, the public has believed the worst about Hollywood. And Jay Leno quipped, "Don't forget Mother's Day. Or as they call it in Beverly Hills, Dad's Third Wife Day."

It's not only comedians like Jay Leno whose late-night monologues have spawned jokes about California, as you'll discover in the "Jokes" chapter. For example, did you hear about the near-tragedy at the mall when there was a power outage? Punchline: Twelve Valley Girls were stuck on the escalators for over four hours. Or that you know you're in California when your child's third-grade teacher has purple hair, a nose ring, and is named Flower . . . and you assume every company offers domestic partner benefits, a fab exercise facility, and tofu take-out.

From the ridiculous we head towards the sublime as the book pays tribute to California's varied scenery. Photographer Ansel Adams called Yosemite Valley, "always a sunrise, a glitter of green and golden wonder in a vast edifice of stone and space" while naturalist John Muir called it, "a place of rest, a refuge from the roar and dust and weary, nervous, wasting work of the lowlands, in which one gains the advantages of both solitude and society."

When it comes to politics, California has always had a roster of controversial and distinctive office-holders. President Ronald Reagan recalled, "I'd been under contract to Warner Brothers for a number of years when [studio head Jack Warner] heard I was running for governor [of California]. I understand that he said, 'No, no. *Jimmy Stewart* for governor. Reagan for best friend." Another actor-turned-governor, Arnold Schwarzenegger, the butt of many jokes (see "Jokes" chapter), has also been recognized for speaking out on serious topics: "There is no better place to be a woman with hopes and dreams than California. The jobs are better paying and more fulfilling and California is a much better place because of that." And when political sniping is the order of the day, consider how Willie Brown, former Mayor of San Francisco, compared ex-Governor Jerry Brown to, "Five-hundred pounds of Jell-O."

No collection of California quotations would be complete without a smorgasbord of memorable lines from and about the state's residents. Among some of my favorites is one by John MacKay, former head coach of the USC Trojans football team, "I'll never be hung in effigy. Before every season I send my men out to buy up all the rope in Los Angeles." Also dealing with sports is one attributed to Earl Warren, California governor who went on to become U.S. Supreme Court Chief Justice, "I always turn to the sports pages first. The sports page records people's accomplishments; the front page nothing but man's failures." And J. Paul Getty's formula for success: "Rise early, work late, and strike oil."

Finally, and by way of acknowledgment, lots of "sweetheart, baby, luv ya, luv ya's" to Californians Liz and Rick Berman, Ardys and Don Burt, Molly and Chris Carpenter, Mari and Rich Goldman, Judy

Goldman, Marnye and Larry Langer, Fred Bauer and Karen Healey, and Ivy Nightingale Russo.

Profound gratitude to Damian Rubino for his contributions to this compilation.

And as ever and fer shur, 1001 thanks and more to my editor Holly Rubino.

STEVEN D. PRICE
NEW YORK, NEW YORK
MARCH 2007

# A State
# So Blessed

*The California Allure*

California here I come, Right back where I started from . . .
> —"*California, Here I Come*," *lyrics and music by Bud De Sylva and Joseph Meyer*

Well, there she is folks. The land of milk and honey—California.
> —*Nunnally Johnson and John Ford, screenplay of* The Grapes Of Wrath

Certainly being in California has encouraged a sustained commitment to rethinking the nature, purposes, and relevance of the contemporary arts, specifically music, for a society which by and large seems to manage quite well without them.
> —*English composer Brian Ferneyhough*

Gold. California's birthstone.

—*journalist Steve Wiegand*

It used to be said that you had to know what was happening in America because it gave us a glimpse of our future. Today, the rest of America, and after that Europe, had better heed what happens in California, for it already reveals the type of civilisation that is in store for all of us.

—*Alistair Cooke*

The attraction and superiority of California are in its days. It has better days and more of them, than any other country.

—*Ralph Waldo Emerson*

The apparent ease of California life is an illusion, and those who believe the illusion will live here in only the most temporary way.

—*Joan Didion*

Right now in California we gain 40,000 new acres of desert every year, with all the building and the people coming in . . . housing going up like crazy.

—*actor Eddie Albert*

I'd like to be able to use Storm's (her super-hero X-men character) powers for good, like have it rain more in Southern California. We could do with it.

—*actress Halle Berry*

California. The sun shines and nothing happens. Before you know it, you're sixty years old.

—*Dudley Nichols, William Faulkner, and Howard Hawks, from the screenplay for* Air Force

The sun shining all the time in November and the grass growing . . . as if we were all shut up in some horrible greenhouse away from the real world and the real seasons.

—*Alison Lurie,* The Nowhere City

I met a Californian who would
Talk California—a state so blessed
He said, in climate, none had ever died there
A natural death . . .

—*Robert Frost, "New Hampshire"*

Look, I live in California. I went to school with a girl called Experience. I had a friend called Breeze. I reckon I got off pretty lightly
—*Chastity Bono, on coping with her first name*

The formula for a happy marriage? It's the same as the one for living in California: when you find a fault, don't dwell on it
—*Jay Trachman*

On nights like that, every booze party ends in a fight. Meek little wives feel the edge of the carving knife and study their husbands' necks.
—*Raymond Chandler, describing the effects of the Santa Ana winds*

Since the gold rush, there may never have been a time when the majority of people living in California were actually born here.
—*James J. Rawles,* California: A Place, A People, A Dream

You haven't lived until you've died in California.
—*Mort Sabl*

The ultimate California bear story is that of the eradication of the grizzly and its reinvention as the proud and ubiquitous emblem of the state, and one of the morals of this story is how quickly such irrevocable loss can happen.
—*Susan Snyder,* Bear In Mind:
The California Grizzly

Everything is just better in California—the wine, the food, fruits and vegetables, the comforts of living. Even the instrumentalists are generous and curious. Everything is wonderful.

—*Beth Anderson*

The California crunch really is the result of not enough power-generating plants and then not enough power to power the power of generating plants.

—*George W. Bush*

When the Oakies left Oklahoma and moved to California, it raised the I.Q. of both states.

—*Will Rogers*

California is where you can't run any farther without getting wet.
—*Neil Morgan*

Every house in the town of the vines has its garden plot, corn and brown beans and a row of peppers reddening in the sun; and in damp borders of the irrigating ditches clumps of yerbasanta, horehound, catnip, and spikenard, wholesome herbs and curative, but if no peppers then nothing at all. You will have for a holiday dinner, in Las Uvas, soup with meat balls and chile in it, chicken with chile, rice with chile, fried beans with more chile, enchilada, which is corn cake with the sauce of chile and tomatoes, onion, grated cheese, and olives, and for a relish chile tepines passed about in a dish, all of which is comfortable and corrective to the stomach. You will have wine which every man makes for himself, of good body and inimitable bouquet, and sweets that are not nearly so nice as they look.
—*Mary Austin*, The Little Town of The Grape Vines

I wish they all could be California girls.
> —"California Girls," lyrics by Mike Love and
> Brian Wilson and sung by The Beach Boys

When California discovered gold, the world discovered California. Willingly or not, as a consequence, Americans were about to learn some sobering and exhilarating truths about themselves.
> —historian Malcolm J. Rohrbough

New Yorkers speak more quickly and shift topics more rapidly . . . The northern California I know isn't like that. Someone talks, and I lie back and listen and let them roll for a while. When they're done, there'll be a pause that will flash like a green light to announce that someone else can have the floor.
> —educator and anthropologist Michael Agar

God never meant man to live here. Man has come and invaded a desert, and he has tortured this desert into giving up sustenance and growth to him, and he has defeated and perverted the purpose of God.

—*Thornton Wilder*

Californians try everything once.

—*T.J. MacGregor*

California is a place in which a boom mentality and a sense of Chekhovian loss meet in uneasy suspension; in which the mind is troubled by some buried but ineradicable suspicion that things had better work here, because here, beneath that immense bleached sky, is where we run out of continent.

—*Joan Didion*

And if California slides into the ocean, as the mystics and statistics say it will, I predict this hotel will be standing until I've paid my bill.
—*Warren Zevon*

Californians say that if you want to eat a Florida orange you have to get into a bathtub first. California oranges are light in weight and have thick skins that break easily and come off in hunks. The flesh inside is marvelously sweet, and the segments almost separate themselves.
—*John McPhee*

As nowhere else, you can fail in California. And I think the California Gold Rush taught people that failure was OK . . . and the result is that people accepted failure, which is the equivalent of saying they are willing to take risks. And California has been the most risk-taking society in the nation, maybe in the world.
—*historian J. S. Holliday*

The only grounds for divorce in California are marriage.

—*Cher*

As one went to Europe to see the living past, so one must visit Southern California to observe the future.

—*Alison Lurie*

California is a tragic country—like Palestine, like every Promised Land. Its short history is a fever-chart of migrations—the land rush, the gold rush, the oil rush, the movie rush, the Okie fruit-picking rush, the wartime rush to the aircraft factories—followed, in each instance, by counter-migrations of the disappointed and unsuccessful, moving sorrowfully homeward.

—*Christopher Isherwood*

Andrea, this is California. Blondes are like the state flower or something.

—*Ian Ziering as Steve Sanders in* Beverly Hills, 90210

It's a scientific fact that if you stay in California you lose one point of your IQ every year.

—*Truman Capote*

Going to California
With an aching in my heart

—*"Going to California," lyrics by Jimmy Page and sung by Led Zeppelin*

It is the land of perpetual pubescence, where cultural lag is mistaken for renaissance.

—*Ashley Montagu*

About the only part of a California house you can't put your foot through is the door. All it did was hurt my shoulder and make me mad.
—*Raymond Chandler,* The Big Sleep

California is a queer place—in a way, it has turned its back on the world, and looks into the void Pacific. It is absolutely selfish, very empty, but not false, and at least, not full of false effort . . . It's sort of crazy-sensible. Just the moment: hardly as far ahead as carpe diem.
—*D.H. Lawrence*

Southern California is a giant sanatorium with flowers, where people come to be cured of life itself in whatever way.

—*John Rechy*, City of Night

Making good wine is a skill. Fine wine is an art.

—*Robert Mondavi*

I looked, there was nothing to see but more long streets and thousands of cars going along them, and dried-up country on each side of the streets. It was like the Sahara, only dirty.

—*Mohammad Mrabet*

Paul Masson. We will sell no wine before its time.

—*advertising slogan for Paul Masson wines*

Californians invented the concept of life-style. This alone warrants their doom.

—*Don DeLillo*

I wouldn't live in California. All that sun makes you sterile.

—*Alan Alda*

Here is a climate that breeds vigour, with just sufficient geniality to prevent the expenditure of most of that vigour in fighting the elements. Here is a climate where a man can work three hundred and sixty-five days in the year without the slightest hint of enervation, and where for three hundred and sixty-five nights he must perforce sleep under blankets. What more can one say? . . . Nevertheless I take my medicine by continuing to live in this climate. Also, it is the only medicine I ever take.

—*Jack London*

I am beginning to think that everyone in California is here by mistake.
—*Woody Allen*

It is a stupid traveler who mocks the ancient wisdom of the country as to what in that country should be eaten. Chiles have been eaten in the region now known as California for thousands of years, a tradition that prudent Californians of modern times should heed.
—*Charles Fletcher Lummis, early twentieth-century author, editor, and preservationist*

Live in New York City once, but leave before it makes you hard.
Live in Northern California once, but leave before it makes you soft.
—*Mary Schmich*

Examine any phase of California life—agriculture, labor, government, industry, social organization, and the examination invariably involves some consideration of the importance of the discovery of gold. Nothing quite like it has ever occurred, or is likely to occur again, in world history.

*—historian Carey McWilliams*

That's okay, this is California. Nobody knows what they're doing, they just smile and fake it.

*—Ian Ziering as Steve Sanders in* Beverly Hills, 90210

Nobody can tell about this California climate. One minute it's hot and the next minute it's cold, so a person never knows what to hock.

*—Anita Loos*

California's a wonderful place to live—if you happen to be an orange.

—*Fred Allen*

To be a California beach bum.

—*Pamela Anderson's ambition as*
*listed in her high school yearbook*

It was one of those clear, bright summer mornings we get in the early spring in California before the fog sets in. The rains are over. The hills are still green and in the valley across the Hollywood hills you can see snow on the high mountains. The fur stores are advertising their annual sales. . . . And in Beverly Hills the jacaranda trees are beginning to bloom.

—*Raymond Chandler*

California, that advance post of our civilization, with its huge aircraft factories, TV and film studios, automobile way of life . . . its favourless cosmopolitanism, its charlatan philosophies and religions, its lack of anything old and well-tried rooted in tradition and character.

—*J.B. Priestley*

In California everyone goes to a therapist, is a therapist, or is a therapist going to a therapist.

—*Truman Capote*

Seems it never rains in Southern California.

—*"It Never Rains In Southern California," lyrics by Albert Hammond and Mike Hazelwood and sung by Albert Hammond*

As a general rule of thumb, however, if you thought of . . .
California as a VCR with nothing to put in, you wouldn't be too far
off the mark.

—*Kinky Friedman*

Chez Panisse began with our doing the very best we could do with
French recipes and California ingredients, and has evolved into
what I like to think of as a celebration of the very finest of our
regional food products. The recipes of Elizabeth David and Richard
Olney provided a starting point and inspiration to us; and we soon
realized that the similarity of California's climate to that of the
south of France gives us similar products that require different
interpretations and executions. My one unbreakable rule has always
been to use only the freshest and finest ingredients available.

—*Alice Waters, co-founder of Chez Panisse,*
*a restaurant known as the birthplace of California cuisine*

There is a theory that almost anything that's fun is going to be ruined sooner or later by people from California. They tend to bring seriousness to subjects that don't deserve it, and they tend to get very good at things that weren't very important in the first place.

—*Calvin Trillin*

A person who can get a good table at Chez Panisse at the last minute is a very important person indeed. Royalty begins with Alice Waters.

—*Willard Speigelman,* Gastronomica *magazine*

California can and does furnish the best bad things that are obtainable in America.

—*Hinton R. Helper*

The devil having been banished and virtue being triumphant,
nothing terribly interesting can ever happen again.
    —*George F. Kennan on California's resemblance to heaven*

You don't have to enjoy being miserable anymore; you're in
California now.
                                            —*Mathew Fisher*

Whether or not the ultimate quality and value of the wines as precisely
as they were found to be on that day, the principle was proven: after
little more than a decade of experience with French techniques,
Californians were able to match the originals they so much admired.
        —*Hugh Johnson*, Vintage: The Story of Wine,
        *when in 1976 at a Paris wine tasting, a California
        red and white were judged the best*

CALIFORNIA: From Latin 'calor', meaning "heat" (as in English 'calorie' or Spanish 'caliente'); and 'fornia', for "sexual intercourse" or "fornication." Hence: Tierra de California, "the land of hot sex."

—*Ed Moran*

California is like an artificial limb the rest of the country doesn't really need. You can quote me on that.

—*Saul Bellow*

In a world in which the influence of the moving image is increasingly ubiquitous, we need to realise what the consequences might be if we fail to offer an alternative to Walt Disney's version of history.

—*Lord David Puttnam*

California, the department store state.

*—Raymond Chandler*

Nothing is wrong with California that a rise in the ocean level wouldn't cure.

*—Ross MacDonald*

I learned more from the one restaurant that didn't work than from all the ones that were successes.

*—Wolfgang Puck, celebrity chef, owner of*
*Spago and other fine California restaurants*

In the South of California has gathered the largest and most miscellaneous assortment of Messiahs, Sorcerers, Saints and Seers known to the history of aberrations.

*—Farnsworth Crowder*

Living in California adds ten years to a man's life. And those extra ten years I'd like to spend in New York.

*—Harry Ruby*

There is science, logic, reason; there is thought verified by experience. And then there is California.

*—Edward Abbey*

He was wearing a hat and a necktie so he couldn't have been in California long.

—*Dorothy Hughes*

It is fatally easy for Western folk, who have discarded chastity as a value for themselves, to suppose that it can have no value for anyone else. At the same time as Californians try to re-invent "celibacy," by which they seem to mean perverse restraint, the rest of us call societies which place a high value on chastity "backward."

—*Germaine Greer*

California is the only state in the union where you can fall asleep under a rose bush in full bloom and freeze to death.

—*W. C. Fields*

Brandy and water.

—*Artemus Ward, the humorist, when asked by the manager of the San Francisco opera house what he would take to lecture for forty nights in California*

California will be a silent place again. It is all as impermanent and brittle as a reel of film.

—*J. B. Priestley*

I lead an introverted and boring life here in California.

—*Brian Bosworth, notorious football player, bad actor, aka "Boz"*

California is an island, and New York's an island. Maybe it's time for me to change islands.

*—actor Paul Mazursky*

If it doesn't get all over the place, it doesn't belong in your face.

*—advertising slogan for Carl's Jr. restaurants,*
*started in Anaheim by Carl Karcher*

I'm happy wherever I go, whatever I do. I'm happy in Iowa, I'm happy here in California.

*—actor Ashton Kutcher*

But the most important thing is, Enron did not cause the California Crisis.

*—the late businessman Kenneth Lay*

In my spare time I hunt for the best fast food places to eat in California! I am a junk food junkie. My favorite is anything I get from Dell Taco.

—*model Cindy Margolis*

And so there I was living in California from Brooklyn, New York and it was this whole new world for me and I was meeting vegetarians. I thought, let me try this vegetarian thing.

—*musician Warren Cuccurullo*

I've been in California for about 15 years now. You're always in your car and insulated. I miss New York so much.

—*actor Jimmy Smits*

I will embrace the first opportunity to get to California and it is altogether probable that when once there I shall never again leave it.

*—George Stoneman*

I did not come to California to fight with a man dressed as Hitler.

*—Borat, [Sasha Baron Cohen] referring to his producer Azamat dressed as Oliver Hardy*

Adultery—which is the only grounds for divorce in New York—is not grounds for divorce in California. As a matter of fact, adultery in southern California is grounds for marriage.

*—musician Allan Sherman*

It is said in the Alps that "not all the vulgar people who come to Chamouny can ever make Chamouny vulgar." For similar reasons, not all the sordid people who drift overland can ever vulgarize California. Her fascination endures, whatever the accidents of population.

*—David Starr Jordan, first president of Stanford University, from California and Californians*

CALIFORNIA is a study. On visiting it, the stranger is, at first, utterly bewildered, finding everything so entirely different from anything he expected or ever saw before. He seems to have alighted on some new planet; the points of compass seem to have swung wrong, and the winds, the trees, the shrubbery, the hills, and valleys, all conspire to confound and mock him, and to enjoy his confusion.

*—Rev. John Todd,* The Sunset Land, *1870*

Had Shakespeare lived in California, he would not have written of the "winter of our discontent," but would most probably have found in the summer of that then undiscovered country a more fitting symbol of the troublous times referred to; for, with the fogs, winds, and dust, that accompany the summer, or the "dry season," as it is more appropriately called in California, it is emphatically a season of discontent.

*—Bishop O.P. Fitzgerald,*
*from* California Sketches, 1860

The Californiac is unable to talk about anything but California, except when he interrupts himself to knock every other place on the face of the earth. He looks with pity on anybody born outside of California and he believes that no one who has ever seen California willingly lives elsewhere.

*—Inez Hayes Irwin, "The Californiacs"*

# II

# THE LONG PASTORAL AGE

A Slice of California History

Know, that on the right hand of the Indies there is an island called California very close to the side of the Terrestrial Paradise; and it is peopled by black women, without any man among them, for they live in the manner of Amazons.

—*Garci Rodríguez de Montalvo*, Las Sergas de Esplandián (The Exploits of Esplandian), *1510*

[This region] is thickly settled with people whom I found to be of gentle disposition, peaceable and docile, and who can be brought readily within the fold of the holy gospel and into subjection to the crown of Your Majesty. The Indians are of good stature and fair complexion, the women being somewhat less in size than the men and of pleasing countenance. The clothing of the people of the coast consists of the skins of the sea-wolves abounding there, which they tan and dress better than is done in Castile; they possess also, in great quantity, flax like that of Castile, hemp and cotton, from which they make fishing-lines and nets for rabbits and hares.

—*explorer Sebastián Vizcaíno, in a 1602 letter to the King of Spain describing Monterey Bay*

It seems to me that there never was a more peaceful or happy people on the face of the earth than the Spanish, Mexican, and Indian population of Alta California before the American conquest. We were the pioneers of the Pacific coast, building towns and Missions while General Washington was carrying on the war of the Revolution, and we often talk together of the days when a few hundred large Spanish ranches and Mission tracts occupied the whole country from the Pacific to the San Joaquin. No class of American citizens is more loyal than the Spanish Californians, but we shall always be especially proud of the traditions and memories of the long pastoral age before 1840.

*—Guadalupe Vallejo, Ranch and Mission Days in Alta California, 1890*

I reached my hand down and picked (the nugget) up; it made my heart thump, for I was certain it was gold.

*—James W. Marshall, discoverer of gold at Sutter's Mill, 1848*

Among the men who remained to hold Sonoma was William B. Ide, who assumed to be in command. In some way (perhaps through an unsatisfactory interview with Frémont which he had before the move on Sonoma), Ide got the notion that Frémont's hand in these events was uncertain, and that Americans ought to strike for an independent republic. To this end nearly every day he wrote something in the form of a proclamation and posted it on the old Mexican flagstaff. Another man left at Sonoma was William L. Todd who painted, on a piece of brown cotton, a yard and a half or so in length, with old red or brown paint that he happened to find, what he intended to be a representation of a grizzly bear. This was raised to the top of the staff, some seventy feet from the ground. Native Californians looking up at it were heard to say 'Coche,' the common name among them for pig or shoat.

—*John Bidwell, on the California*
*Republic flag of 1846*

I saw the first gold ever discovered in California. Marshall came over to our house in Benicia and stayed all night. He was on his way to San Francisco from Sutter's mill. He said he thought he had gold. He took out a little rag that looked like the bit of a bag that housewives keep aniseed in and opened it. We all looked at it in wonder.

—Mrs. Susan Wolfskill, *later reiminiscing on the discovery*

I looked on for a moment; a frenzy seized my soul; unbidden my legs performed some entirely new movements of Polka steps—I took several—houses were too small for me to stay in; I was soon in the street in search of necessary outfits; piles of gold rose up before me at every step; castles of marble, dazzling the eye with their rich appliances; thousands of slaves, bowing to my beck and call; myriads of fair virgins contending with each other for my love, were among the fancies of my fevered imagination. The Rothschilds, Girards and Astors appeared to me but poor people; in short, I had a very violent attack of the Gold Fever.

—James H. Carson, *on being shown a sack of gold nuggets in* 1848

Gold Mountain.

*—Nineteenth century Chinese immigrants'*
*name for California*

A scramble of needy adventurers . . . and a general jail delivery of all the rowdies of the river.

*—Ralph Waldo Emerson, on the Gold Rush*

There is a stocky John Bull, a Chinaman, a Hindu, a Russian, and a native Californio, all trying to converse. A Chilean and an Oregonian are watching each other suspiciously. A Frenchman and an Italian are winking at a Hawaiian girl crowned with flowers and clad in a blue dress and red shoes.

*—Vincente Perez Rosales, a Chilean diarist*
*observing people drawn to the Gold Rush*

I sluiced many and many a day. One member of our party picked up a $400 nugget on the Honecut. There were no bakeshops in those early days, and I made many an apple pie, just of common dried apples, and sold them for a dollar apiece. The women helped in that way to support the families, for mining was not always a certain means of livelihood.

—*Mrs. Noble Martin, reminiscing on her gold-mining days*

The California fever is not likely to take us off . . . . There is neither romance nor glory in digging for gold after the manner of the pictures in the geography of diamond washing in Brazil.

—*Rutherford B. Hayes*

Many, [California pioneers] after long days of suffering—and death—were rolled in a blanket and laid to rest, with nothing more solemn than the lifting of hats. They left no record. And only the wind sighing a requiem through the trees is left of their earthly heritage. Even at this late day remnants of their insignia, or craft (shovels, picks and pans) may be found. For time, the destroyer of all things earthly, has swept aside "with the Pioneer his tradition, his trails and landmarks" into oblivion. A few lived their allotted span of life, where they dug for gold; others went glimmering with things that were, and a very few live to tell the tale.

—*Mrs. Lee Whipple-Haslam,*
Early Days in California, *1920*

The gold-digger in the ravines of the mountains is as much a gambler as his fellow in the saloons of San Francisco. What difference does it make whether you shake dirt or shake dice? If you win, society is the loser.

—*Henry David Thoreau*

The Old Dry Diggings or, rather, the Log Cabin Ravine, was the first mining camp I was in, and though it is 22 years ago, it is still fresh in my memory. It was to me more like a pleasure party than anything else. No one worked very hard; everyone had great hopes; and round our campfires at night we would pass pleasant evenings, singing and spinning yarns. Not a quarrel took place, or fight, while I was camped there. Neither was there many there who drank liquor to excess. As it was my first mining experience, so likewise it was, taking it in all, the happiest, as I saw no blows struck while there.

*—John A. Hussey, a trip to the gold mines of California in 1848*

I came from Salem City
with my washpan on my knee
I'm going to California,
the gold dust for to see.

*—49ers "theme song" set to the tune of Stephen Foster's "Oh Susanna"*

If I must be cast in destitution on the care of a stranger, let it be in California, but let it be before the American avarice has hardened the heart and made a god of gold.

*—Walter Colton, contemporary*
*observer of the 49ers*

The majority—four-fifths, we believe—of the inhabitants of California are opposed to slavery. They believe it to be an evil and a wrong . . . and while they would rigidly and faithfully protect the vested rights of the South, they deem it a high moral duty to prevent its extension and aid its extinction by every honorable means.

*—editorial,* Alta California, *1849*

I regard education as a subject of particular importance here in California, from our location and the circumstances under which we are placed, the immense value of our lands and the extent and wealth of the country.

*—delegate Robert Semple at the first Constitutional Convention of California in 1849*

[W]ith the exception of what we got the Mission of Santa Barbara, native wine, that we tasted, was such trash as nothing but politeness could have induced us to swallow.

*—Sir George Simpson of the Hudson's Bay Company on early California wine-making efforts*

Providence was particularly unkind to the [wine] growers of Anaheim. In 1885 a mysterious disease hit their vines like the plagues of Egypt. Today we know that "Anaheim disease" is a bacterial infection. In the 1880's it was simply a message to move north.

—*Hugh Johnson,* Vintage: The Story of Wine

In April 1850, the newly chartered California state legislature, known as the "Legislature of a Thousand Drinks" for its prolific consumption of booze during the hard-rain winter they first convened, passed the Foreign Miners' Tax Law. The bill assessed a $20 per month levy on any claim held by a non-citizen. It was, of course, only selectively enforced, first on the Chinese miners, who were nearly defenseless, since they were not trained to use rifles.

—*historian Steven Lavoie, "Miss Liberty"*

Those citizens of San Francisco at the outbreak of the Civil War were far more patriotic American citizens than were those who some years before, at Sonoma, had declared for a California republic and hoisted a bear flag instead of that of the country from which they had emigrated into a foreign country. The same amount of cloth would have made for those a flag in the similitude of the Stars and Stripes. They did not make one.

The men of San Francisco and California in 1860 did not want any flag but that of the American Republic. They honored that flag too much to substitute for it anything else. Some of them had made the long, good fight to have the new land of their endeavor represented by a new star on that flag.

—*Charles Beebe Turrill,*
California Notes, *1876*

My own opinion is that California is the best state in the American Republic for business at all times and under all circumstances. But you, who have lived here, can require only this additional information. If in time of peace California possessed advantages superior to all other American states, now, in time of the insane war, it possesses no rival. It must be the most desirable of all states in every particular, for a residence, during the war. It never was more prosperous than it is today.

*—William J. Shaw, letter to the*
*American envoy in Guatemala, 1864*

Those who fail to visit California this year [1915] miss an opportunity the like of which will not recur in a lifetime.

*—from a Union Pacific Railway booklet on how to*
*get to the Panama-Pacific International Exposition*

There is not in all California an institution of greater public convenience than that of Wells, Fargo & Co.'s Express. It is endeared to our people by a thousand associations, dating from the present back to early pioneer times. It has long supplied, and still supplies a necessity peculiar to the nomadic characteristics of a mining people . . . In such cases, mail and express facilities are needed, and are always supplied by Wells, Fargo & Co., with an energy and efficiency that has won the admiration of all visitors to this coast, and has secured the undying gratitude of our own people. It is an institution of which Californians are justly proud.

—San Francisco News Letter and
California Advertiser, 1880

[T]he Southern Pacific Railroad, [was] the corporation that swung California by its golden tail, that controlled its legislature, its farmers, its preachers, its workers.

—*Mary H. Jones*

Every city on earth has its special sink of vice, crime and degradation, its running ulcer or moral cancer, which it would fain hide from the gaze of mankind. . . . San Franciscans will not yield the palm of superiority to anything to be found elsewhere in the world. Speak of the deeper depth, the lower hell, the maelstrom of vice and iniquity—from whence those who once fairly enter escape no more forever—and they will point triumphantly to the Barbary Coast, strewn from end to end with the wrecks of humanity, and challenge you to match it anywhere outside of the lake of fire and brimstone.

—*Col. Albert S. Evans, A la California:*
*Sketch of Life in the Golden State, 1873*

Oranges for Health—California for Wealth.

—*slogan of a 1907 advertising campaign to*
*attract Iowans to move to California to*
*work in the citrus-growing industry*

Whenever the stage stopped to change horses, we would wake up, and try to recollect where we were . . . . We began to get into country, now, threaded here and there with little streams. These had high, steep banks on each side, and every time we flew down one bank and scrambled up the other, our party inside got mixed somewhat. First we would all be down in a pile at the forward end of the stage, nearly in a sitting posture, and in a second we would shoot to the other end, and stand on our heads. And we would sprawl and kick, too, and ward off ends and corners of mailbags that came lumbering after us and about us; and as the dust rose from the tumult, we would all sneeze in chorus, and the majority of us would grumble, and probably say some hasty thing, like: "Take your elbow out of my ribs!—Can't you quit crowding."

—*Mark Twain, on stagecoach travel*
*in California, circa 1851*

The moment an incoming ship touches the wharf, the "runners" of these leeches are on hand with their wagons to carry off the easily seduced sailors. Once the sailor reaches the boarding-house, he occupies the same position toward the "boarding-master" that the fly does toward the spider in whose net it has been caught. He is at once filled up with vile whisky, and carefully kept in that state. His wages—and he generally pays off with $100 and upwards—are taken by the "boarding-master" "for safe-keeping," and he is judiciously supplied with a few dollars occasionally "to spend outside the house." At the end of a couple of weeks he is gently informed that his money is all gone, and it is time for him to go to sea again.

—San Francisco News Letter, 1881,
*on the practice of acquiring sailors as crew members*

People began to understand that with the acquisition of California the nation had obtained practically half a continent, of which the future possibilities were almost unlimited . . .

—*nineteenth-century businessman John Moody*

In their native states, the Americans are practically a versatile people. There must be some new word found to express how inexhaustible their resources become in California.

—*Eliza Farnham*, California, In-doors and Out, *1856*

The "curiosities" of the earthquake were simply endless. Gentlemen and ladies who were sick, or were taking a siesta, or had dissipated till a late hour and were making up lost sleep, thronged into the public streets in all sorts of queer apparel, and some without any at all. One woman who had been washing a naked child, ran down the street holding it by the ankles as if it were a dressed turkey. Prominent citizens who were supposed to keep the Sabbath strictly, rushed out of saloons in their shirt-sleeves, with billiard cues in their hands.

—*Mark Twain, on the 1865 San Francisco earthquake*

[E]very suggestion that Mr. Evarts [a California plumber turned gold miner] gave me turned to gold. He advised me to take a chance at the head of a couple of abandoned gulches. In both cases I struck it rich enough to add $6,000 to my working capital. Again he suggested a lease of a hydraulic mine on what was known as Railroad Hill, which had been the ruin of several experienced miners. I followed his advice and after being brought to the verge of bankruptcy struck it rich, to my way of thinking, and cleaned up finally with $60,000 to my credit, all before my 17th birthday.

—*Asbury Harpending, California Pioneer, from* The Great Diamond Hoax and Other Stirring Episodes in the Life of Asbury Harpending, *edited by James H. Wilkins*

"Look here, Mr. King," he said. "This is the bulliest diamond field as never was. It not only produces diamonds, but cuts them moreover also."

—*a man to Clarence King, the geologist who exposed the great diamond hoax of 1872, from Asbury Harpending, California Pioneer, from* The Great Diamond Hoax and Other Stirring Episodes in the Life of Asbury Harpending, *edited by James H. Wilkins*

But what an awakening! You must know that I am not a very heavy sleeper—I always wake early, and when I feel restless I get up and go for a walk. So on the Wednesday morning early I wake up about 5 o'clock, feeling my bed rocking as though I am in a ship on the ocean, and for a moment I think I am dreaming that I am crossing the water on my way to my beautiful country. And so I take no notice for the moment, and then, as the rocking continues, I get up and go to the window, raise the shade and look out. And what I see makes me tremble with fear. I see the buildings toppling over, big pieces of masonry falling, and from the street below I hear the cries and screams of men and women and children.

*—opera singer Enrico Caruso, on the 1906*
*San Francisco earthquake and fire*

. . . unhesitating, fierce, joyful embrace of the awful force of nature . . . of contact with elemental reality.

*—William James' reaction to the 1906 earthquake*

On the morning of the 18th of April I was awakened from a sound slumber by a terrific trembling, which acted in the same manner as would a bucking broncho. I sat up in bed with a start. My bed was going up and down in all four directions at once, while all about me I heard screams, wails, and crashing of breaking china-ware and nick-nacks. I was very quietly watching the clock on the mantel, which was doing a fancy stunt, while the ornaments in the parlor could be heard crashing to the floor.

*—piano maker Peter Bacigalupi,*
*on the 1906 San Francisco earthquake and fire*

When I came out to California, Bill, some blamed idiot who knew it all, advised me what to bring. He said—(and I'll bet my old pair of suspenders he never saw California) says he, "Don't take any winter clothes out there with you, its such a hot country you wont need 'em. " Wall, I didnt, and by gum, I like to froze to death.

*—Mina Deane Halsley,* A Tenderfoot in
Southern California, *1909*

Old John Dimming, "Honest John" as his patrons used to call him, has stabled his nag for the last time. The famous hackman has surrendered to the taxicab, and his weather-beaten vehicle will be seen no more in Powell Street. It was inevitable. The cab made a heart-breaking stand against the motor; the night hawk refused to retire before the chauffeur. But it looks as though the end has come. Who hires a hack these days, except for a funeral? Almost nobody. The prices are higher than taxi rates, and the pace is much too slow for this speeding age.

—The Pacific Weekly, *1914*

In San Francisco, before the fire of 1906, people lived in homes of anywhere from eight to ten or twelve rooms, or flats of six or eight rooms. After the fire, there was a necessity of immediate dwellings, and many of the burned buildings were replaced with new cliff-dwellings or apartment houses, because they took up less space and housed more people. Some of the homes also were given over to this same purpose, and after the exposition more apartments were built, and the cliff-dwellers were in San Francisco to stay.

—The WASP, *1918*

Whereas the University was founded in memory of our dear son, Leland, and bears his name, I direct that the number of women attending the University as students shall at no time ever exceed 500 . . . . I mean literally never in the future of the Leland Stanford Junior University can the number of female students at any one time exceed 500.

*—Jane Stanford, founder with her husband Leland of Stanford University, 1899 (her directive remained in effect until 1933)*

The meaning of our movement to End Poverty In California [his so-called EPIC movement] and its polling the largest vote ever cast in a California primary, is that our people have reached the saturation point as regards suffering. We are just about to begin the sixth year of the depression. We have one-and-a-quarter million persons dependent upon public charity, and probably as many more who are able to get only one or two days' work a week or who are dependent upon relatives and friends. That is too heavy a burden of suffering for any civilized community to carry.

*—Upton Sinclair, author and candidate for governor, 1934*

The Second Gold Rush: Wartime ship-building in the East Bay.

*—source unknown*

California was wide open—experimental, innovative and exceptionally creative environment. People felt free to try new ideas, anything at all.

*—Paul Horn commenting on post-World War II California*

Here were students being dragged by their hair, dragged by their arms and legs down the stairs so that their head were bouncing off the stairs. That was the start of the Sixties for me.

*—Betty Denitch on "Black Friday" in San Francisco, May 1960*

Employers are going to love this generation. . . . They are going to be easy to handle. There aren't going to be any riots.
—*Clark Kerr, president of the University of California at Berkeley, 1963*

. . . the mesmerizing vision of a white kids' car-and-surf-based Utopia.

—*Mike Davis on the California "surfing sound" pop music of the '60s*

I don't think that the California myth, the dream that a few of us touched, would have happened without Brian [Wilson], but I don't think Brian would have happened without the dream.
—*songwriter Jimmy Webb on The Beach Boys' lead singer*

If you're going to San Francisco, be sure to wear flowers in
your hair.

—*Scott McKenzie*

I got to San Francisco and found everybody dressed up in 1890s
garb . . . they had a more "rustic-than-thou" approach. It was cute,
but it wasn't as evolved as what was going on in L.A.

—*musician Frank Zappa*

We were doing the Monterey Pop Festival, which I produced with
Lou Adler, and the town of Monterey was sort of frightened by the
thought of two hundred and fifty thousand hippies coming.

—*John Phillips, of The Mamas and the Papas*

The vibe was beautiful. The music was fantastic. To me, that was the purest, most beautiful moment of the whole sixties trip.

—*Dennis Hopper on the 1967 Monterey Pop Festival*

Today's Pig Is Tomorrow's Bacon.

—*newspaper headline in California, 1968*

Here's the man who doesn't have any identity. But tonight he has the Los Angeles Police Department and the Los Angeles Fire Department upset. He has the National Guard called out. Tonight he is somebody.

—*a black minister during the Watts Riots in Los Angeles in 1965*

Sew the rags of surplus into teepees.

> —*a leaflet passed out in Haight-Ashbury in the '60s*

. . . our smiles are our political banners and our nakedness is our picket sign!

> —*Berkeley activist Jerry Rubin*

There is a time when the operation of the machine becomes so odious, makes you so sick at heart, that you can't take part . . . and you've got to put your bodies upon the gears . . . and you've got to make it stop.

> —*Mario Savio, leader of the*
> *Berkeley Free Speech Movement*

All of this began the first time some of you who know better—and are old enough to know better—let young people think that they have the right to choose laws they would obey as long as they were doing it in the name of social protest.

—*Ronald Reagan to University of California faculty members, as quoted in the film* Berkeley in the Sixties

The Third Gold Rush: Silicon Valley.

—*source unknown*

# III

# THE TREASURE VEINS

*California in Literature*

The great bulk of writing done in California records the impressions of people born and educated thousands of miles from the Golden Gate, and estimating life by standards widely different from those generally current on California and Market streets, or commonly accepted on Nob Hill and Pacific Avenue. Their work is, therefore, not in any strict sense Californian literate. And, now that the impulse given to the imagination by the picturesque ante-Gringo period and "the days of gold" has pretty well died out, it is not easy to see just what direction the literary activity of California will take. Californian literature has had its Golden Age, and it is not unreasonable to expect that for many years to come there will be nothing specifically distinctive about it.

—San Francisco News Letter, 1897

Tho the dark be cold and blind,
Yet her sea-fog's touch is kind,
And her mightier caress
Is joy and the pain thereof;
And great is thy tenderness,
O cool, grey city of love!
    —*George Sterling, "The Cool, Grey City of Love," the lines*
    *appear on a tablet in a Russian Hill park in San Francisco*

Cannery Row in Monterey in California is a poem, a stink, a grating
noise, a quality of light, a tone, a habit, a nostalgia, a dream. Cannery
Row is the gathered and scattered, tin and iron and rust and splintered
wood, chipped pavement and weedy lots and junk heaps, sardine
canneries of corrugated iron, honky tonks, restaurants and whore
houses, and little crowded groceries, and laboratories and flophouses.
    —*John Steinbeck,* Cannery Row

And what a brilliant sight it was! The flowers had faded on the hills, for June was upon them; but gayer than the hills had been was the race-field of Monterey. Caballeros, with silver on their wide gray hats and on their saddles of embossed leather, gold and silver embroidery on their velvet serapes, crimson sashes about their slender waists, silver spurs and buckskin botas, stood tensely in their stirrups as the racers flew by, or, during the short intervals, pressed each other with eager wagers. There was little money in that time. The golden skeleton within the sleeping body of California had not yet been laid bare. But ranchos were lost and won; thousands of cattle would pass to other hands at the next rodeo; many a superbly caparisoned steed would rear and plunge between the spurs of a new master.

—*Gertrude Franklin Horn Atherton, "The Pearls of Loreto"*

Al: Ain't you gonna look back, Ma? Give the old place a last look? Ma Joad: We're goin' to California, ain't we? Alright then, let's go to California.

—*John Steinbeck,* The Grapes Of Wrath

The Bay of Monterey has been compared by no less a person than
General Sherman to a bent fishing-hook; and the comparison, if less
important than the march through Georgia, still shows the eye of a
soldier for topography. Santa Cruz sits exposed at the shank; the
mouth of the Salinas river is at the middle of the bend; and
Monterey itself is cosily ensconced beside the barb. Thus the
ancient capital of California faces across the bay, while the Pacific
Ocean, though hidden by low hills and forest, bombards her left
flank and rear with never-dying surf.

—*Robert Louis Stevenson*, Across the Plains

Great on the west, ere darkness crush her domes,
Wine-red the city of the sunset lies.
Below her courts the mournful ocean foams;
Above, no foam of cloud is in the skies.
—*George Sterling, "The Evanescent City," written on the closing
of San Francisco's Panama-Pacific International Exposition,
which ran from February through December, 1915*

The [San Francisco] street never failed to interest him. It was one of those cross streets peculiar to Western cities, situated in the heart of the residence quarter, but occupied by small tradespeople who lived in the rooms above their shops. There were corner drug stores with huge jars of red, yellow, and green liquids in their windows, very brave and gay; stationers' stores, where illustrated weeklies were tacked upon bulletin boards; barber shops with cigar stands in their vestibules; sad-looking plumbers' offices; cheap restaurants, in whose windows one saw piles of unopened oysters weighted down by cubes of ice, and china pigs and cows knee deep in layers of white beans.

—*Frank Norris*, McTeague

I've been as bad an influence on American literature as anyone I can think of.

—*Dashiell Hammett, San Francisco founder of the "hard-boiled" school of detective novel writing*

The valley framed by mountains of purplish gray, dull brown, with
patches of vivid green and yellow; a solitary gray peak, barren and
rocky, in sharp contrast to the rich Californian hills; on one side
fawn-coloured slopes, and slopes with groves of crouching oaks in
their hollows; opposite and beyond the cold peak, a golden hill
rising to a mount of earthy green; still lower, another peak, red and
green, mulberry and mould; between and afar, closing the valley,
a line of pink-brown mountains splashed with blue.

*—Gertrude Atherton,*
*The Conquest of Dona Jacoba*

Not all proud Sheba's queenly offerings,
Could match the golden marvel of thy blooms.
For thou art nurtured from the treasure veins
Of this fair land; thy golden rootlets sup
Her sands of gold—of gold thy petals spun.

*—Ida Coolbrith, "The California Poppy"*

It is difficult for a European to imagine Calistoga, the whole place is so new, and of such an accidental pattern; the very name, I hear, was invented at a supper-party by the man who found the springs.

—*Robert Louis Stevenson*, The Silverado Squatters

The Salinas Valley is in Northern California. It is a long narrow swale between two ranges of mountains, and the Salinas River winds and twists up the center until it falls at last into Monterey Bay.

—*John Steinbeck*, East of Eden

What peaches and what penumbras! Whole families shopping at night! Aisles full of husbands! Wives in the avocados, babies in the tomatoes!—and you, Garcia Lorca, what were you doing down by the watermelons?

—*Alan Ginsberg*, "A Supermarket in California"

. . . this Berkeley was like no somnolent Siwash out of her own past at all, but more akin to those Far Eastern or Latin American universities you read about, those autonomous culture media where the most beloved of folklores may be brought into doubt, cataclysmic of dissents voiced, suicidal of commitments chosen— the sort that bring governments down.

—*Thomas Pynchon,* The Crying of Lot 49

Like other Berkeley radicals, he [Rodman, the main character's son] is convinced that the post-industrial post-Christian world is worn out, corrupt in its inheritance, helpless to create by evolution the social and political institutions, the forms of personal relations, the conventions, the moralities, and systems if ethics insofar as these are indeed necessary) appropriate to the future.

—*Wallace Stegner,* Angle of Repose

A few miles south of Soledad, the Salinas River drops in close to the hillside bank and runs deep and green. The water is warm too, for it has slipped twinkling over the yellow sands in the sunlight before reaching the narrow pool.

—*John Steinbeck*, Of Mice and Men

The Monterey of last year exists no longer. A huge hotel has sprung up in the desert by the railway. Three sets of diners sit down successively to table. Invaluable toilettes figure along the beach and between the live oaks; and Monterey is advertised in the newspapers, and posted in the waiting-rooms at railway stations, as a resort for wealth and fashion. Alas for the little town! it is not strong enough to resist the influence of the flaunting caravanserai, and the poor, quaint, penniless native gentlemen of Monterey must perish, like a lower race, before the millionaire vulgarians of the Big Bonanza.

—*Robert Louis Stevenson*, Across the Plains

It was the last half of September, the very end of the dry season, and all Tulare County, all the vast reaches of the San Joaquin Valley—in fact all South Central California, was bone dry, parched, and baked and crisped after four months of cloudless weather, when the day seemed always at noon, and the sun blazed white hot over the valley from the Coast Range in the west to the foothills of the Sierras in the east.

—*Frank Norris*, The Octopus

Nor will [he] ever again hear the sea lions
Grunt in the kelp at Point Lobos.
Nor look to the south when the grunion
Run the Pacific, and the plunging
Shearwaters, insatiable,
Stun themselves in the sea.

—*William Everson, "The Poet Is Dead,"*
*from a memorial for Robinson Jeffers*

"You want to know why California wine is not drunk in the States?" a San Francisco wine merchant said to me, after he had shown me through his premises. "Well, here's the reason."

And opening a large cupboard, fitted with many little drawers, he proceeded to shower me all over with a great variety of gorgeously tinted labels, blue, red, or yellow, stamped with crown or coronet, and hailing from such a profusion of CLOS and CHATEAUX, that a single department could scarce have furnished forth the names. But it was strange that all looked unfamiliar.

"Chateau X-?" said I. "I never heard of that."

"I dare say not," said he. "I had been reading one of X-'s novels."

—*Robert Louis Stevenson, "Napa Wines"*

Leadville made its appearance as a long gulch . . . littered with wreckage, shacks, and mine tailings. It was rutted deep by ore wagons, scalped of its timber. The smoke of smelters and charcoal kilns smudged a sky that all down the pass had been a dark, serene blue.

—*Wallace Stegner,* Angle of Repose

Just where the track of the Los Gatos road streams on and upward like the sinuous trail of a fiery rocket until it is extinguished in the blue shadows of the Coast Range, there is an embayed terrace near the summit, hedged by dwarf firs. At every bend of the heat-laden road the eye rested upon it wistfully; all along the flank of the mountain, which seemed to pant and quiver in the oven-like air, through rising dust, the slow creaking of dragging wheels, the monotonous cry of tired springs, and the muffled beat of plunging hoofs, it held out a promise of sheltered coolness and green silences beyond.

—*Bret Harte, "Flip—A California Romance"*

The rain! The rain! The generous rain!
All things are his who knows to wait.
Behold the rainbow bends again
Above the storied, gloried Gate—
God's written covenant to men
In tyrian tins on cloth of gold,
Such as no tongue or pen hath told!

—*Joachin Miller, "California's Resurrection"*

Grant Avenue, the main street and spine of this strip, is for most of its length a street of gaudy shops and flashy chop-suey houses, catering to the tourist trade, where the racket of American jazz orchestras drowns the occasional squeak of a Chinese flute.
> —*Dashiell Hammett, "Dead Yellow Women"*

But not even the soft wash of dusk could help the houses. Only dynamite would be of any use against the Mexican ranch houses, Samoan huts, Mediterranean villas, Egyptian and Japanese temples, Swiss chalets, Tudor cottages, and every possible combination of these styles that lined the slopes of the canyon.
> —*Nathaniel West,* The Day Of The Locust

O'er Carmel fields in the springtime the sea-gulls follow the plow.
White, white wings on the blue above!
White were your brow and breast, O Love!
But I cannot see you now.
Tireless ever the Mission swallow
Dips to meadow and poppied hollow;
Well for her mate that he can follow,
As the buds are on the bough.

—*George Sterling, "Spring in Carmel"*

. . . instead I've bounced drunk into his City Lights bookshop at the
height of Saturday night business . . . and 't'all ends up a roaring
drunk in all the famous bars the bloody 'King of the Beatniks' is
back in town buying drinks for everyone . . .

—*Jack Kerouac, "Big Sur"*

Cold steamy air blew in through two open windows, bringing with it half a dozen times a minute the Alcatraz foghorn's dull moaning. A tinny alarm-clock, insecurely mounted on a corner of Drake's Celebrated Criminal Cases of America—face down on the table— held its hands at five minutes past two.

—*Dashiell Hammett*, The Maltese Falcon

From Shasta town to Redding town
The ground is torn by miners dead;
The manzanita, rank and red,
Drops dusty berries up and down
Their grass-grown trails. Their silent mines
Are wrapped in chaparral and vines;
Yet one gray miner still sits down
Twixt Redding and sweet Shasta town.

—*Joachin Miller, "The Gold That Grew By Shasta Town"*

. . . luxuriant gardens
with flowers as big as trees, which of course would wither
Hesitently if not nourished with very expensive water.

—*Berthold Brecht*

What shall be said of the sun-born Pueblo?
This town sudden born in the path of the sun?
This town of St. James, of the calm San Diego,
As suddenly born as if shot from a gun?

—*Joachin Miller, "San Diego"*

On soft Spring nights I'll stand in the yard under the stars—
Something good will come out of all things yet—And it will be
golden and eternal just like that—There's no need to say another word.

—*Jack Kerouac, "Big Sur"*

Reagan's Homeless kept getting in the way
of Downtown Southern California Traffic.
—*Rod McKuen, "The Winter of Eighty-Eight"*

~

I was an old man by the time I took that walk to the Public Library
in San Francisco, because the years between birth and twenty are
the years in which the soul travels farthest and swiftest.
—*William Saroyan,* The Bicycle Rider in Beverly Hills

~

For me there is only the traveling on the paths that have heart,
on any path that may have heart. There I travel, and the only
worthwhile challenge for me is to traverse its full length. And
there I travel—looking, looking, breathlessly.
—*Carlos Casteneda in the voice of Don Juan Matus,*
The Teachings of Don Juan: A Yaqui Way of Knowledge

~

The fog lay thick on the bay at dawn next morning. The white waves hid the blue, muffled the roar of the surf. Now and again a whale threw a volume of spray high in the air, a geyser from a phantom sea. Above the white sands straggled the white town, ghostly, prophetic.

*—Gertrude Atherton, "The Pearls of Loreto"*

At the end of our streets is sunrise;
At the end of our streets are spars;
At the end of our streets is sunset;
At the end of our streets the stars.

*—George Sterling, "The City By the Sea"*

# IV

# SEVENTY-TWO SUBURBS IN SEARCH OF A CITY

Los Angeles

L.A.: Come on vacation, go home on probation.

*—crime novelist James Ellroy*

The final story, the final chapter of western man, I believe, lies in Los Angeles.

*—Phil Ochs*

I don't want to move to a city where the only cultural advantage is being able to make a right turn on a red light.

*—Woody Allen, in* Annie Hall

In Los Angeles, everyone is a star.

*—Denzel Washington*

This town makes no demands on you, and offers you everything good. It's all here—the best facilities and the best climate.

*—Derek Taylor, The Beatles' sometimes press officer*

Los Angeles makes the rest of California seem authentic.

*—Jonathan Culler*

Los Angeles is seventy-two suburbs in search of a city.

—*Dorothy Parker*

In Los Angeles, there is so much money and power connected with ostentation that it is no longer ludicrous: it commands a kind of respect. For if the mighty behave like this, then quiet good taste means that you can't afford the conspicuous expenditures, and you become a little ashamed of your modesty and propriety.

—*critic Pauline Kael*

[Los Angeles was] a place of motorized transience, where not only relationships but the landscape was fickle and unenduring.

—*Peter Conrad*, Imagining America

What I hate about L.A. is that you have to seem young, happy and successful all the time.

*—anonymous television producer*

The freeway experience . . . is the only secular communion Los Angeles has. . . . Actual participation requires a total surrender, a concentration so intense as to seem a kind of narcosis, a rapture-of-the-freeway. The mind goes clean. The rhythm takes over.

*—Joan Didion*

We live in Los Angeles, where you are expected to move every two to four years, so people can see how well your career is going.

*—Rita Rudner*

In Los Angeles, by the time you're thirty-five, you're older than most of the buildings.

—Delia Ephron

Los Angeles is just New York lying down.

—Quentin Crisp

Eat in the hat.

—neon sign atop the first Brown Derby
restaurant on Wilshire Boulevard, Los Angeles

So few human contacts in Los Angeles go unmediated by glass
(either a TV screen or an automobile windshield), that the direct
confrontation renders the participants docile, stunned, sweet.

—*Edmund White*

From Mount Hollywood, Los Angeles looks rather nice, enveloped
in a haze of changing colors. Actually, and in spite of all the
healthful sunshine and ocean breezes, it is a bad place—full of old,
dying people, who were born old of tired pioneer parents, victims
of America—full of curious wild and poisonous growths, decadent
religious cults and fake science, and wildcat enterprises, which, with
their aim for quick profit, are doomed to collapse and drag down
multitudes of people.

—*Louis Adamic*

Fall is my favorite season in Los Angeles, watching the birds change color and fall from the trees.

—*David Letterman*

Isn't it nice that people who prefer Los Angeles to San Francisco live there?

—*Herb Caen*

So, I live in Los Angeles, and it's kind of a goofy place. They have an airport named after John Wayne. That ought to explain it. It has a charming kind of superstitious innocence.

—*George Carlin*

If most American cities are about the consumption of culture, Los Angeles and New York are about the production of culture—not only national culture but global culture.

—*Barbara Kruger, artist*

I used to like this town. Los Angeles was just a big dry sunny place with ugly homes and no style. Now we've got the big money, the sharp shooters, the percentage workers, the fast-dollar boys, the hoodlums out of New York and Chicago . . .

—*Raymond Chandler,* The Little Sister

When it's 100 degrees in New York, it's 72 in Los Angeles. When it's 30 degrees in New York, in Los Angeles it's still 72. However, there are 6 million interesting people in New York, and 72 in Los Angeles.

—*Neil Simon*

I love Los Angeles. I love Hollywood. They're beautiful. Everybody's plastic, but I love plastic. I want to be plastic.

—*Andy Warhol*

The town is like an advertisement for itself; none of its charms are left to the visitor's imagination . . .

—*Christopher Isherwood*

Pick your enemies carefully or you'll never make it in Los Angeles.

—*Rona Barrett*

I like it [L.A.] much better than I used to, probably because I like New York much less. As New York has gotten duller and duller, L.A. seems less awful. I doubt very much that L.A. has become less awful, it's just that in contrast to New York it seems less awful. You never have to have human contact here; there are very few actual humans to have contact with.

—*Fran Lebowitz*

I am beginning to appreciate Los Angeles. True, Frank Lloyd Wright [or was this Dorothy Parker or H.L. Mencken?] called it a lot of suburbs looking for a city (he also said: the United States tilts to the southwest and everything loose ended up in Southern California), and I still resent the long drives on the freeways. But I now feel this is the only large cosmopolitan city where I can be warm all year, close by the sea and still create my own paradise just five minutes from downtown.

—*Anais Nin*

If you spend any time in Los Angeles, there's only one topic of conversation.

*—actor Alan Rickman*

In Los Angeles, four to five cars follow you every day, everywhere you go. Is it really that interesting?

*—Kate Hudson*

Rodeo Drive is a giant Butterscotch Sundae.

*—Andy Warhol, on the Beverly Hills shopping district*

I was street-smart—but unfortunately the street was Rodeo Drive.
—*Carrie Fisher*

L.A. I liked because the degenerates there all stay in their separate suburban houses.
—*Paul Morrisey, director of Andy Warhol's movies*

When I came to Los Angeles, it was the first time that I ever felt like I belonged somewhere. Not because it was wacky, but because people here understood what I felt like to perform, and there were other kids my age who wanted to do it. I didn't get looked at as God, you freak.
—*Jennifer Love Hewitt*

In New York you can whine and complain, and everybody lets it roll off because they accept ups and downs. In L.A. if you're negative, you get treated as if you have some sort of emotional cancer and people are scared to be near you.

—*anonymous television producer*

In the house in Beverly Hills where our four children grew up, living conditions were a few thousand times improved over the old tenement on New York's East 93rd Street we Marx Brothers called home.

—*Harpo Marx*

If you stay in Beverly Hills too long, you become a Mercedes.

—*Robert Redford*

Went to Los Angeles for several days to write the titles for motion pictures. Lost five days from my novel and tired myself in the bargain.

—*Zane Grey*

. . . Los Angeles is a constellation of plastic . . .

—*Norman Mailer,* Miami and the Siege of Chicago

I read the Life magazine articles about free love and free dope in California. At age 20 I drove to Los Angeles.

—*rock musician Glenn Frey*

If one stopped the flow of water here for three days, the jackels
would reappear.

—*film writer Hanns Eisler*

European imperialism long ago made Tahiti a distant suburb of
Paris, the missionaries made it a suburb of Christ's kingdom, and the
radio made it a suburb of Los Angeles.

—*sociologist Cedric Belfrage*

We were on the beach in Los Angeles communicating with the sun.

—*rock musician Ray Manzarek*

Downtown Los Angeles is at present one of the most squalid places in the United States.

—*Christopher Isherwood*

In Los Angeles versus the San Gabriel Mountains, it is not always clear which side is losing.

—*John McPhee*, Rising from the Plains

Los Angeles has of course been called every name in the book, from "nineteen suburbs in search of a metropolis" to a "circus without a tent" to "less a city than a perpetual convention."

—*John Gunther*, Inside U.S.A.

Los Angeles has the greatest concentration of surviving movie palaces in the United States, yet most residents have never been inside one of them.

—*Leonard Maltin*

I'd move to Los Angeles if New Zealand and Australia were swallowed up by a tidal wave, if there was a bubonic plague in England and if the continent of Africa disappeared from some Martian attack.

—*Russell Crowe*

I think it's only right that crazy people should have their own city, but I cannot for the life of me see why a sane person would want to go there.

—*Bill Bryson,* The Lost Continent

Thank God I don't live in Los Angeles. I think if you're there
the whole time it just gets out of proportion and you lose touch
completely with reality.

*—British film director Sam Mendes*

The first time I reported on Los Angeles two agronomists took
me on a long drive to Riverside to show me the danger line where
orange trees would no longer grow because of smog and the line
closer to the city where spinach, more sensitive than man,
blackened and withered in the atmosphere Los Angeles breathed.

*—Harrison E. Salisbury,* Travels Around America

I'm a Valley Girl. You can't get me out of the Valley, I'm still here.

*—model Cindy Margolis*

Between a quarter and a third of Los Angeles's land area is now monopolized by the automobile and its needs—by freeways, highways, garages, gas stations, car lots, parking lots. And all of it is blanketed with anonymity and foul air.

—*Alistair Cooke*

The violet hush of twilight was descending over Los Angeles as my hostess, Violet Hush, and I left its suburbs [and] headed towards Hollywood. In the distance a glow of huge piles of burning motion-picture scripts lit up the sky. The crisp tang of frying writers and directors whetted my appetite. How good it was to be alive, I thought, inhaling deep lungfulls of carbon monoxide.

—*S.J. Perelman*, Strictly from Hunger

I love Los Angeles. It reinvents itself every two days.

—*Billy Connolly*

Study as hard as you can and if you are serious Los Angeles is the place for television and movies and New York for theater.

—*Sela Ward*

Los Angeles is a microcosm of the United States. If L.A. falls, the country falls.

—*Ice T*

This is the city. Los Angeles, California. I work here. I carry a badge. My name's Friday. The story you are about to see is true; the names have been changed to protect the innocent.
—*Jack Webb as Sgt. Joe Friday in the radio and TV series* Dragnet

You can have a laugh in Los Angeles, or you can weep in Los Angeles, depending on your attitude towards it.
—*Miranda Richardson*

There we were, renting a Mustang convertible and driving down Sunset [Boulevard] picking up beautiful blonde girls . . . If anything, I got an overly golden impression of Los Angeles at that point.
—*Peter Asher, of the '60s British rock duo Peter and Gordon*

When you're in Los Angeles, nobody bats an eye, they're so used to seeing actors, they just act really cool.

*—actor Luke Wilson*

That's pretty much how Los Angeles views me—I'm on a par with serial killers.

*—actress Sherry Stringfield*

Because this is a show biz town, you could put together a band with a look, a feel, a sound, and the entertainment value was taken for granted.

*—music publisher Dan Bourgoise*
*commenting on The Monkees*

Australia is so cool that it's hard to even know where to start describing it. The beaches are beautiful; so is the weather. Not too crowded. Great food, great music, really nice people. It must be a lot like Los Angeles was many years ago.

—*actress Mary-Kate Olsen*

The whole city gives you the impression of impermanence. You have the feeling that one day someone is going to yell. "Cut! Strike it!" and then the stagehands will scurry out and remove the mountains, the movie-star homes, the Hollywood Bowl—everything.

—*comedian-musician Allan Sherman*

Los Angeles is a much better theater town than it ever gets credit for—there's a lot of good theater out there.

—*director Michael Ritchie*

If there were a major earthquake in Los Angeles, with bridges
and highways and railroads and airports all shut down and huge
buildings collapsing, I don't care how much planning you do, the
first 72 hours is going to be chaotic.

*—Senator Warren Rudman*

Los Angeles is not a town full of airheads. There's a great deal of
wonderful energy there.

*—actor Alan Rickman*

When they show the destruction of society on color TV, I want
to be able to look out over Los Angeles and make sure they get
it right.

*—Phil Ochs*

In Los Angeles, it's like they jog for two hours a day and then they think they're morally right. That's when you want to choke people, you know?

—*Liam Neeson*

The difference between Los Angeles and yogurt is that yogurt comes with less fruit.

—*Rush Limbaugh*

And people get mad all the time [in New York]. When people don't like something, like "Get out of my way you blah, blah, blah." But [in L.A.] it's like, "How ya doing? Let's do lunch! I love you!"

—*musician Jeff Buckley*

Los Angeles is a large city-like area surrounding the Beverly Hills Hotel.

—*Fran Liebowitz*

Cities are distinguished by the catastrophic forms they presuppose and which are a vital part of their essential charm. New York is King Kong, or the blackout, or vertical bombardment: Towering Inferno. Los Angeles is the horizontal fault, California breaking off and sliding into the Pacific: Earthquake.

—*Jean Baudrillard*

I noticed I had developed a fantasy about myself as a writer as opposed to actually doing it [so] I finally summoned up the bad taste to move to Los Angeles.

—*Leslie Dixon*

I'm in Los Angeles today;
garbage cans comprise the medians
of freeways always creeping
even when the population's sleeping.
And I can't see why you'd want to live here.
                    —"Why You'd Want to Live Here"
                    by the group Death Cab for Cutie

Paris got the Seine. Vienna's got the Blue Danube. L.A.'s got a . . .
concrete drainage ditch. It's all we've got. It'll have to do.
                    —dialogue from the short-lived TV show
                    Boomtown, referring to the L.A. River

Either you bring the water to L.A. or you bring L.A. to the water.
                    —Noah Cross, played by actor
                    John Huston, from the movie Chinatown

. . . Los Angeles, or Southern California as a whole, constitutes a social world of its own that is peculiarly disordered, speeded up, and artificial. The popular idea (substantiated to a degree by historians) is that because California was for so long the special end point of the westering dream, the pot of gold at the end of the rainbow of hopes of countless pioneers, it has received more than its share of restless visionaries and misfits and is therefore a more intensely neurotic version of the neurotic life of modern America.

—*Janis P. Stout,* The Journey Narrative in American Literature

. . . I drive down to Wilshire and then onto Santa Monica and then I drive onto Sunset and take Beverly Glen to Mulholland, and then to Sepulveda to Ventura and then I drive through Sherman Oaks to Encino and then into Tarzana and then Woodland Hills. I stop at Sambo's that's open all night . . .

—*Bret Easton Elllis, in the voice of the main character, Clay, from the novel* Less Than Zero

To live sanely in Los Angeles (or, I suppose, in any other large American city) you have to cultivate the art of staying awake. You must learn to resist (firmly but not tensely) the unceasing hypnotic suggestions of the radio, the billboards, the movies and the newspapers; those demon voices which are forever whispering in your ear what you should desire, what you should fear, what you should wear and eat and drink and enjoy, what you should think and do and be.

*—Christopher Isherwood*

People cut themselves off from their ties of the old life when they come to Los Angeles. They are looking for a place where they can be free, where they can do things they couldn't do anywhere else.

*—former mayor Tom Bradley*

# V

# THE
# WESTERN
# GATE

San Francisco

San Francisco—this is a derivative word from sand and Francisco. In the early settlement of this country it was the custom of an old monk of the interior, by the name of Jeremiah Francisco, to perform a pilgrimage to this place every month, to visit the tomb of a brother of the order whose remains he had here interred. The wind "blew like mad" here, and upon his return he was usually so covered with the dust and sand, that his neighbors were unable to recognize him; hence they soon began to call him sand Francisco. On one of his pilgrimages he happened, by mistake, to die here, and the place ever after was called by his name. From the difficulty of enunciating the d, it was usually called SAN FRANCISCO, and has so continued to this day. The present popular notion that the place was named after the St. Francis Hotel is an error!

—California Weekly Courier, 1850

From this tableland, one enjoys a most delicious view; for from there one observes a good part of the bay and its islands as far as the other side, and one has a view of the ocean as far as the Farallones. In fact, although, so far as I have traveled, I have seen very good places and beautiful lands, I have yet seen none that pleased me so much as this. I do believe that, if we could be well populated, as in Europe, there would be nothing more pretty in the world; for this place has the best accommodations for founding on it a most beautiful city, inasmuch as the desirable facilities exist as well on the land as on the sea, the port being exceptional and capacious for dockyards, docks, and whatever would be wanted.

*—Father Font, on viewing*
*San Francisco Bay in 1776*

You wouldn't think such a place as San Francisco could exist.
The wonderful sunlight there, the hills, the great bridges, the Pacific
at your shoes. Beautiful Chinatown. Every race in the world. The
sardine fleets sailing out. The little cable-cars whizzing down
The City hills. And all the people are open and friendly.

—*Dylan Thomas*

Nob Hill in San Francisco has long been a symbol of the city's
elegance and grace. Known originally as the California Street Hill,
it became the home of San Francisco's wealthiest families in the
1870s. The city's elite were the "nabobs," (referring to the title of
prominent governors of the Mogul empire in India) which was later
shortened simply to "nobs."

—*Californiahistory.net*

Every quarter of the city discharged its residents into the broad
procession. Ladies and gentlemen of imposing social repute; their
German and Irish servant girls, arms held fast in the arms of their
sweethearts; French, Spaniards, gaunt, hard-working Portugese;
Mexicans, the Indian showing in reddened skin and high cheekbone
—everybody, anybody, left home and shop, hotel, restaurant, and
beer garden to empty into Market Street in a river of color. Sailors
of every nation deserted their ships at the water front and, hurrying
up Market Street in groups, joined the vibrating mass excited by the
lights and stir and the gaiety of the throng. "This is San Francisco,"
their faces said.

*—Harriet Lane Levy*, 920 O'Farrell Street

Somehow the great cities of America have taken their places in a
mythology that shapes their destiny: Money lives in New York.
Power sits in Washington. Freedom sips Cappuccino in a sidewalk
cafe in San Francisco.

*—Joe Flower*

Serene, indifferent of Fate,
Thou sittest at the Western Gate;
Upon thy height, so lately won,
Still slant the banners of the sun;
Thou seest the white seas strike their tents,
O Warder of two continents!
And, scornful of the peace that flies
Thy angry winds and sullen skies,
Thou drawest all things, small or great,
To thee, beside the Western Gate.

—*Bret Harte, "San Francisco"*

I think San Francisco is the best place in the whole world for an easy life.

—*photographer Imogen Cunningham*

I fell in love with the most cordial and sociable city in the Union.

—*Mark Twain*

[Following the discovery of gold, San Francisco was] a great place,
such a one as the world never produced before, crowded with
people from all parts of the world, the Yankees & the Chinaman
(sic) jostling each other in the streets, while French, Germans,
Sandwich Islands, Chillians (sic), Malays, Mexicans, &c &c
in all their varieties of costume and language go to form a
"congrommoration" of humanity, such as the world never saw before.

—*Rinaldo Taylor, a visiting Bostonian in 1849*

In San Francisco, Halloween is redundant.

—*comedian Will Durst*

Nearly everybody in San Francisco writes poetry. Few San Franciscans would admit this, but most of them would rather like to have their productions accidentally discovered.

*—Stella Benson*

Careful now. We're dealing here with a myth. This city is a point upon a map of fog; Lemuria in a city unknown. Like us, It doesn't quite exist.

*—Ambrose Bierce*

San Francisco is a mad city—inhabited for the most part by perfectly insane people whose women are of a remarkable beauty.

*—Rudyard Kipling*

Here we are all paupers together, but we have our grit left.
—*Ernest H. Adams, to his Boston employer following*
*the San Francisco earthquake and fire in 1906*

. . . everyone is an artist, but their masterpiece is their identity inscribed on their body and displayed in public with pride, whether it's a leatherman wrapped in gym-generated muscle mass and cowhide or a slacker so covered in tattoos she looks like the Sunday funnies or the various neo-tribals with their dreadlocks and baggies or the bicyclist wearing a "One Less Car" t-shirt or, for that matter, the street preachers holding their corner at Sixteenth and Mission or Fifth and Market (where a man with a "no unlawful sex" sandwich-board has been preaching his own peculiar gospel for more than a decade).

—*Rebecca Solnit*

San Francisco was where the social hemorrhaging was showing up.
San Francisco was where the missing children were gathering and
calling themselves "hippies."

—*Joan Didion, Slouching Towards Bethlehem*

San Francisco is simply beautiful. It is a perfectly delightful
company, all very enthusiastic and young and eager.

—*Vivien Leigh*

East is East, and West is San Francisco, according to Californians.
Californians are a race of people; they are not merely inhabitants
of a State.

—*O. Henry*

I love San Francisco and I love you fans. My family knows, God knows, I'm proud to wear this uniform.

—*Barry Bonds*

Most of the men on the Comstock were burrowing in the ground that they might live on Nob Hill, overlooking the Golden Gate. When Mark Twain, as he lay awake imagining himself a millionaire, told his bedfellow that the first thing he was going to do with his money was to build a castle in San Francisco, he was expressing succinctly the close relationship between Washoe and the metropolis of the West.

—*Franklin Walker, Literary Frontier*

I have always been rather better treated in San Francisco than I actually deserved.

—*Mark Twain*

San Francisco is a city where people are never more abroad than when they are at home.

—*Benjamin F. Taylor*

There are hardly any left in New York City. The San Francisco Bay Area is very fortunate to still have a lot of independent bookstores.

—*Lawrence Ferlinghetti*

When the Chinese first came to San Francisco, they were actually welcomed by the mayor and they had special ceremonies for them—again this is when their colony was very small, only a few Chinese.

—*historian Iris Chang*

My history is San Francisco.

*—Barry Bonds*

⌢

What I wanted most was a steady job in San Francisco, year round.

*—Dave Brubeck*

⌢

We had a lot of fun seeing the sights of Frisco, especially the Barbary Coast. In those days [the 1910s] it was full of spots such as Purcell's, the hot colored joint, and the Cave, which San Franciscans boasted was the toughest place in the world. I was keen to see and hear the entertainers there so we made up a party to go one night after the show. We had a guide because we had been told it wasn't safe to "do" the Barbary Coast without one.

*—entertainer Sophie Tucker*

⌢

Col. Cobb: Yes, but San Francisco is no place for a woman.
Swan: Why not? I'm not afraid. I like the fog. I like this new world.
I like the noise of something happening. . . . I'm tired of dreaming,
Colonel Cobb. I'm staying. I'm staying and holding out my hands
for gold—bright, yellow gold.

*—Ben Hecht and Charles MacArthur,*
*screenplay for* Barbary Coast

San Francisco is a city of startling events. Happy is the man whose
destiny it is to gather them up and record them in a daily newspaper!

*—Mark Twain*

There may not be a Heaven, but there is a San Francisco.

*—Ashley Brilliant*

San Francisco is an interesting place. It's always been such a nice culturally diverse environment, which it still is, but there's a lot of money there now and a lot of dot com's so it's a little different than it used to be.

*—musician Les Claypool*

Old San Francisco, which is the San Francisco of only the other day, the day before the Earthquake, was divided midway by the Slot. The Slot was an iron crack that ran along the center of Market Street, and from the Slot arose the burr of the ceaseless, endless cable that was hitched at will to the cars it dragged up and down. In truth, there were two slots, but in the quick grammar of the West time was saved by calling them, and much more that they stood for, "The Slot." North of the Slot were the theaters, hotels, and shopping district, the banks and the staid, respectable business houses. South of the Slot were the factories, slums, laundries, machine-shops, boiler works, and the abodes of the working class.

*—Jack London, "South of the Slot"*

[California] is the land where the fabled Aladdin's Lamp lies buried—and [San Francisco] is the new Aladdin who shall seize it from its obscurity and summon the genie and command him to crown her with power and greatness and bring to her feet the hoarded treasures of the earth.

—*Mark Twain*

If, as they say, God spanked the town
For being over-frisky,
Why did He burn all the churches down
And spare Hotaling's Whiskey?

—*popular song by Charles K. Field,*
*on the survival of a local distillery during*
*the 1906 San Francisco earthquake.*

They were a wonderful set of burglars, the people who were running
San Francisco when I first came to town in 1923, wonderful because,
if they were stealing, they were doing it with class and style.

—*Sally Stanford, well-known madam*

I have seen few things as beautiful as a 6:30 A.M. lift-off from
San Francisco International Airport in the autumn. From above,
the rippled fog layer laps against the shores of the foothills like a
voluminous cotton ocean.

—*photographer Eric Cheng*

It is an odd thing, but every one who disappears is said to be seen
at San Francisco. It must be a delightful city, and possess all the
attractions of the next world.

—*Oscar Wilde*

Drop down, O fleecy Fog and hide
Her skeptic sneer, and all her pride!
—Bret Harte, "San Francisco from the Sea"

San Francisco is where gay fantasies come true, and the problem the city presents is whether, after all, we wanted these particular dreams to be fulfilled—or would we have preferred others.
—author Edmund White

You can never go without a coat in the summer in the city of San Francisco.
—Mark Twain

Chicago is the great American city, New York is one of the capitals of the world, and Los Angeles is a constellation of plastic; San Francisco is a lady.

—*Norman Mailer*

You can go one block to the next in San Francisco and get a completely different opinion of what the issue is.

—*actor Don Johnson*

No city invites the heart to come to life as San Francisco does. Arrival in San Francisco is an experience in living.

—*William Saroyan*

A "Bay Area Bisexual" told me I didn't quite coincide with either of her desires.

—*Woody Allen*

I'm going to do what every San Franciscan does who goes to Heaven. I'll look around and say, "It's not bad, but it ain't San Francisco."

—*Herb Caen*

Coming of age in San Francisco I was often ashamed of my parents and resisted their downhome ways. In my view they were Okies, and I was not an Okie. I was born in the city by the Golden Gate, where you saved your paper-route money to buy cashmere sweaters.

—*writer James D. Houston*

San Francisco has long been called the most European of American cities, a comment more often made than explained. What I think its speakers mean is that San Francisco is, in its scale and its street life, something like the original idea of a city as a place of unmediated encounters, while most of the rest of the cities of the American West are more like enlarged suburbs . . .

—*Rebecca Solnit*

Several centuries from now perhaps there will be an added footnote, when some learned researcher or scholar will attempt to tell how people in San Francisco lived. The future encyclopedia will read something like this: "The city is built on a flock of hills, skirted by the ocean. On each of these hills—some of the ninety-five degree angle variety—are so-called dwellings of anywhere from eight to ten tiers, or floors. Each of these tiers is divided into several small compartments, in which people live, exist or reside.

—The WASP, *1918*

Where else but in San Francisco would characters such as Sister Boom-Boom, a transvestite who dresses in a miniskirted nun's habit, and a punk rocker named Jello Biafra run for seats on the Board of Supervisors? And where else would 75,000 runners dress like centipedes, gorillas, and six packs of beer to participate in the "moving masquerade ball" otherwise known as the Bay to Breakers Race?

—*JoAnne Davidson*

San Francisco has always been my favorite booing city. I don't mean the people boo louder or longer, but there is a very special intimacy. When they boo you, you know they mean you. Music, that's what it is to me. One time in Kezar Stadium they gave me a standing boo.

—*Chicago Bears football coach George Halas*

What fetched me instantly [about San Francisco] (and thousands of other newcomers with me) was the subtle but unmistakable sense of escape from the United States.

—*H. L. Mencken*

Money monopoly has reached its grandest proportions. Here, in San Francisco, the palace of the millionaire looms up above the hovel of the starving poor with as wide a contrast as anywhere on earth.

—*politican and labor organizer Dennis Kearney*

I will sing in San Francisco if I have to sing in the streets, for I know that the streets of San Francisco are free.

—*opera diva Luisa Tetrazzini*

There may not be a Heaven, but there is a San Francisco.
*—English author and cartoonist Ashleigh Brilliant*

[San Francisco] . . . the city that never was a town.
*—Will Rogers*

The Golden Gate Bridge's daily strip tease from enveloping stoles of mist to full frontal glory is still the most provocative show in town.
*—journalist Mary Moore Mason*

If you're alive, you can't be bored in San Francisco. If you're not
alive, San Francisco will bring you to life.

—*William Saroyan*

Perpetual spring, the flare of adventure in the blood, the impulse
of men who packed Virgil with their bean-bags on the overland
journey, conspired to make San Francisco a city of artists.

—*William Henry Irwin*

When you get tired of walking around San Francisco, you can
always lean against it.

—*anonymous*

To a Christian who has toiled months and months in Washoe;
whose hair bristles from a bed of sand, and whose soul is caked with
a cement of alkali dust; whose nostrils know no perfume but the
rank odor of sage-brush—and whose eyes know no landscape but
barren mountains and desolate plains; where the winds blow, and
the sun blisters, and the broken spirit of the contrite heart finds joy
and peace only in Limburger cheese and lager beer—unto such a
Christian, verily the Occidental Hotel [in San Francisco] is Heaven
on the half shell.

—*Mark Twain*

There are just three big cities in the United States that are "story
cities"—New York, of course, New Orleans, and, best of the lot,
San Francisco.

—*Frank Norris*

San Francisco itself is art, above all literary art. Every block is a short story, every hill a novel. Every home a poem, every dweller within immortal. That is the whole truth.

*—William Saroyan*

I was married once—in San Francisco. I haven't seen her for many years. The great earthquake and fire in 1906 destroyed the marriage certificate. There's no legal proof. Which proves that earthquakes aren't all bad.

*—W. C. Fields*

San Francisco is perhaps the most European of all American cities.

*—Cecil Beaton*

Once I knew the city very well, spent my attic days there, while others were being a lost generation in Paris, I fledged in San Francisco, climbed its hills, slept in its parks, worked on its docks, marched and shouted in its revolts. It had been home to me in the days of my poverty and it did not resent my temporary solvency.

—*John Steinbeck*

Nothing important has ever come out of San Francisco, Rice-a-Roni aside.

—*Michael O'Donoghue*

Those who survived the San Francisco earthquake said, "Thank God, I'm still alive." But, of course, those who died, their lives will never be the same again.

—*Senator Barbara Boxer*

There is always inequity in life. Some men are killed in a war and
some men are wounded, and some men never leave the country, and
some men are stationed in the Antarctic and some are stationed in
San Francisco . . . Life is unfair.

*—John F. Kennedy*

I have seen purer liquors, better segars, finer tobacco, truer guns and
pistols, larger dirks and bowie knives, and prettier courtesans here in
San Francisco than in any other place I have ever visited; and it is
my unbiased opinion that California can and does furnish the best
bad things that are available in America.

*—Hinton Helper*

Let us go and talk with the poets.

*—Joaquin Miller, on arriving in San Francisco*

Sir, I view the proposal to hold an international exhibition at San Francisco with an equanimity bordering on indifference.

—*Sir William S. Gilbert*

I used to travel in tennis shoes; I am just not allowed to anymore. I'm an old hippie from San Francisco.

—*Amy Irving*

Many of the evils which afflicted the people of San Francisco may be traced to the peculiar circumstances attendant upon the settlement of California. The effect all over the world of the discovery of gold at Sutter's Mill in 1848 was electric. A movement only paralleled by that of the Crusades at once commenced. Adventurers of every character and description immediately started for the far away land where gold was to be had for the gathering.

—*Stephen Palfrey Webb, Mayor of San Francisco 1854-55*

I prefer San Francisco to Los Angeles. . . . Why? The kind of concentration . . . creates certain choices, an openness of society that is not possible in the lower-density environments.

—*architect Moshe Safdie*

The San Francisco Stock Exchange was the place that continuously pumped up the savings of the lower classes into the pockets of the millionaires.

—*Robert Louis Stevenson*

It is hardly fair to blame America for the state of San Francisco, for its population is cosmopolitan and its seaport attracts the floating vice of the Pacific; but be the cause what it may, there is much room for spiritual betterment.

—*Sir Arthur Conan Doyle*

I'd never set foot in San Francisco. Of all the Sodoms and Gomorrahs in our modern world, it is the worst. There are not 10 righteous (and courageous) men there. It needs another quake, another whiff of fire—and—more than all else—a steady trade wind of grapeshot . . . . That moral penal colony of the world.

—*Ambrose Bierce*

I never saw so many well-dressed, well-fed, business-looking Bohemians in my life.

—*Oscar Wilde, on the Bohemians Club*

A madhouse of frenzied moneymaking and frenzied pleasure-seeking, with none of the corners chipped off. It is beautifully situated and the air reminds one curiously of Edinburgh.

—*Aleister Crowley, written in 1898*

The old charm had vanished completely. It had become a regular
fellow. The earthquake had swallowed up romance, and the fire
burnt up the soul of the city to ashes. The phoenix had perished
and from the cinders had arisen a turkey buzzard.

*—Aleister Crowley, again in 1917*

There they are at last, Miss Rutledge. The will-o-the-wisps with
plagues of fortune. San Francisco, the latest newborn of a great
republic.

*—Ben Hecht and Charles MacArthur,*
*screenplay for* Barbary Coast

The City that knows how.

*—William Howard Taft*

In San Francisco, vulgarity, "bad taste," [and] ostentation are regarded as a kind of alien blight, an invasion or encroachment from outside.

—*critic Pauline Kael*

Truly it is only those who place all happiness in money who could submit, for the sake of gain, to live in such a place.

—*world traveler Ida Pfeiffer*

The San Francisco Bay Area [is] the playpen of countercultures.

—*R. Z. Sheppard*

Myself, both times I have gone to California, I have vowed to see Yosemite, the big trees, the string of beautiful old missions which dot the state, some of the quaint, languid, semi-tropical towns of the south, some of the brisk, brilliant, bustling towns of the north. But I have never really done it because I saw San Francisco first.

—*Inez Hayes Irwin, "The Californiacs"*

You look back and see how hard you worked and how poor you were, and how desperately anxious you were to succeed, and all you can remember is how happy you were.

—*Jack London, recalling his youth in San Francisco*

San Francisco is a golden handcuff with the key thrown away.

—*John Steinbeck*

San Francisco beats the world for novelties; but the inventive faculties of her people are exercised on a specialty. Controversy is our forte.

—San Francisco Call, *September 15, 1864*

San Francisco is the longest lasting love affair of my life. Her beauty inspires me anew each day and I am very thankful to be able to live here on the edge of the continent in what I feel is the heart beat of the world.

—*source unknown*

The extreme geniality of San Francisco's economic, intellectual and political climate makes it the most varied and challenging city in the United States.

—*James Michener*

It's simply a very romantic place. Just one look at any of those streets, and you couldn't be anywhere else—it's so beautiful, and there's that location, and the sense of the free spirit. Who couldn't become ravenous in such a place?

—*Julia Child*

We're crazy about this city. First time we came here, we walked the streets all day, all over town and nobody hassled us . . . Los Angeles? That's just a big parking lot where you buy a hamburger for the trip to San Francisco.

—*John Lennon*

The Bay Area is so beautiful, I hesitate to preach about heaven while I'm here.

—*Billy Graham*

I love this city. If I'm elected, I will move the White House to San Francisco. I went to Fisherman's Wharf and they even let me into Allioto's. It may be Baghdad by the Bay to you, but to me it's Resurrection City.

—*Robert Kennedy*

The ultimate [travel destination] for me would be one perfect day in San Francisco. There's no city like it anywhere. And, if I could be there with the girl of my dreams, that would be the ultimate!

—*Larry King*

I have done more for San Francisco than any other of its old residents. Since I left there it has increased in population fully 300,000. I could have done more—I could have gone earlier—it was suggested.

—*Mark Twain*

I always see about six scuffles a night when I come to San Francisco. That's one of the town's charms.

—*Errol Flynn*

You are fortunate to live here. If I were your president, I would levy a tax on you for living in San Francisco.

—*Mikhail Gorbachev*

San Francisco is one of the great cultural plateaus of the world—one of the really urbane communities in the United States—one of the truly cosmopolitan places and for many, many years, it always has had a warm welcome for human beings from all over the world.

—*Duke Ellington*

I'm proud to have been a Yankee. But I have found more happiness and contentment since I came back home to San Francisco than any man has a right to deserve. This is the friendliest city in the world.

—*Joe DiMaggio*

Maybe it [San Francisco] felt so much the opposite of L.A. and that feeling like you were cut loose in a grid of life that just spilled out to the edge of everything.

—*William Gibson,* Virtual Light

Your city is remarkable not only for its beauty. It is also, of all the cities in the United States, the one whose name, the world over, conjures up the most visions and more than any other, incites one to dream.

—*French president Georges Pompidou*

I don't know of any other city where you can walk through so many culturally diverse neighborhoods, and you're never out of sight of the wild hills. Nature is very close here.

—*poet Gary Snyder*

San Francisco is 49 square miles surrounded by reality.

—*Paul Kanter, of the rock band Jefferson Airplane*

But oh, San Francisco! It is and has everything—you wouldn't think that such a place as San Francisco could exist. The lobsters, clams, crabs. Oh, Cat, what food for you. And all the people are open and friendly.

—*Dylan Thomas*

I came out to California from Texas, to the Haight, and the Fillmore and all that stuff, and totally got the bug.

—*musician Christopher Cross*

As many of you know, I come from San Francisco. We don't have a lot of farms there. Well, we do have one—it's a mushroom farm, so you know what that means.

—*Speaker of the House Nancy Pelosi to the Agribusiness Club of Washington, July 24, 2006*

San Francisco, I believe, has the most disagreeable climate and locality of any city on the globe.

—*Eliza Farnham,* California, In-doors and Out, *1856*

So you just call it [San Francisco] "The City." Oh, right, "The City."
And Oakland's just a collection of houses, is it?
—*British comedian Eddie Izzard*

The things that spell San Francisco to me are disappearing fast. I should
have liked to have lived here then—color, excitement, power, freedom.
—*Galvin Elster, played by actor Tom Helmore,
from the movie* Vertigo

A Californiac once made the statement to me that Californians
considered themselves a little better than the rest of the country. I
considered that the prize Californiacism until I heard the following
from a woman-Californiac in Europe: "I saw nothing in all Italy,"
she said, "to compare with the Italian quarter of San Francisco."
—*Inez Hayes Irwin, "The Californiacs"*

Madame World was a wise mother when she chose this spot
for her Fair.

> —*Elizabeth Gordon, What We Saw at*
> *Madame World's Fair, on San Francisco's*
> *Panama-Pacific Exposition of 1915*

Thus pouring into California in every direction and by every route,
this strange and heterogeneous mass of men, the representatives of
every occupation, honest and dishonest, creditable and disgraceful;
of every people under the sun, scattered through the gulches and
ravines in the mountains, or grouped themselves at certain points in
cities, towns and villages of canons or adobe. Perhaps never in the
world's history did cities spring into existence so instantaneously,
and certainly never was their population so strangely diverse in
language, habits and customs.

> —*Stephen Palfrey Webb,*
> *Mayor of San Francisco 1854-55*

San Francisco is noted for its hilly streets. One morning as I was
coming to my office on a Sutter street car, and like most men
silently thinking, and worrying about certain problems I was to face
during the day, I looked ahead at the high hills our car was going
to have to climb, and I wondered how power enough could be
generated to push it over the tops of them. As we came to them, it
seemed as though they had disappeared, and we were traveling on
level ground. That evening as I rode home, I tried to call to mind
some of the worries I carried down with me that morning but
they, like the hills, had disappeared as I came to them.

—*Coleman Cox*, Listen to This

The Human Be-In was publicized as a "Gathering of the Tribe,"
but it was actually more a gathering of the suburbs with only a
sprinkling of nonwhites in the crowd of three hundred thousand.

—*author Emmett Grogan on 1967's*
*"Human Be-In" in San Francisco*

San Francisco in the middle sixties was a very special time and place to be a part of. Maybe it meant something. Maybe not, in the long run . . . There was a fantastic universal sense that whatever we were doing was right, that we were winning . . . There was no point in fighting—on our side or theirs. We had all the momentum; we were riding the crest of a high and beautiful wave . . . . So now, less than five years later, you can go up on a steep hill in Las Vegas and look West, and with the right kind of eyes you can almost see the high-water mark—that place where the wave finally broke and rolled back.

—*H. S. Thompson*, Fear and Loathing in Las Vegas

San Francisco has only one drawback. 'Tis hard to leave.

—*Rudyard Kipling*

Please remember as you approach Haight Street that you are about to see one of the most wondrous sights yet to come to the attention of mankind. . . . Many tourists upon seeing the unshaven, unconventionally clothed Love Generation roll up their car windows and lock their doors. This is not necessary and can be mighty inconvenient. Some of the hippies do bite, but all of them have taken their rabies shots so their bite is not too bad.

—*Haight-Ashbury Maverick*, 1967

Leaving San Francisco is like saying goodbye to an old sweetheart. You want to linger as long as possible.

—*Walter Cronkite*

# VI

# THE CHOSEN SPOTS

The Smaller Towns and Cities of California

The chosen spot of all this earth.
—*Luther Burbank on Santa Rosa*

White sand, white sky, white people.
—*Richard Meltzer on Newport Beach*

Twenty-six miles across the sea. Santa Catalina is waiting for me.
—*"Twenty-six Miles," lyrics and music*
*by Glen Larson and Bruce Belland*

I think maybe L.A. or San Francisco could be rushed, but
Sacramento is just laid back!

*—baseball player Nick Johnson*

Few people who had come of age with Napa Valley had escaped
without scars.

*—James Conaway,* Napa

What was the use of my having come from Oakland it was not
natural to have come from there yes write about it if I like or
anything if I like but not there, there is no there there.

*—Gertrude Stein*

In contrast to Yankee Mendocino, the well-protected little dog-hole of Bodega Bay is more like a Mediterranean village, with its population of Italian and Portuguese fishermen who still spread their nets along the docks for inspection and repair.

*—Walter Cronkite,* Around America

If Carmel's founders should return, they could not afford to live there, but it wouldn't go that far. They would be instantly picked up as suspicious characters and deported over the city line.

*—John Steinbeck,* Travels with Charley

The rottenest city on the Pacific Coast.

*—Earl Warren on Emeryville,*
*said before his election as governor in 1942*

Beyond a procession of gaudy signboards, gas stations, and
roadstands, are scattered suburban bungalows; in nearby vacant
lots, family goats feed on yellow buttercups in the spring.

*—El Cerrito, as described in*
The WPA Guide to California, *1939*

⌒

Like other southern California valley towns in the early thirties,
[El Monte] was gradually and unintentionally passing from a rural
community into something else, undecided as yet but full of
one-story stucco houses and small businesses, with a chain
five-and-dime and two modest movie palaces.

*—Leonard Nathan*, California Childhood

⌒

The light, the dry, always refreshing warmth; the spaciousness,
the ocean . . .

*—Thomas Mann on Santa Monica*

⌒

La Jolla, perched as it is on a spectacular bluff, is one of those picture-perfect California resort cities. Its architecture is determinedly Cal-Mex, and its atmosphere is genteel rich.

*—Walter Cronkite*, Around America

During those years in Oildale, the mid-1940s, I needed only to walk across the street to find a patch of virgin desert.

*—Gerald Haslam*, California Childhood

Ojai was, still is, a small dusty town twenty miles inland from the California everybody knows, the California of postcards.

*—Valerie Hobbs*, California Childhood

Pacific Grove and Monterey sit side by side on a hill bordering the bay. The two towns touch shoulders but they are not alike. Whereas Monterey was founded a long time ago by foreigners, Indians and Spaniards and such, and the town grew up higgledy-piggledy without plan or purpose, Pacific Grove sprang full blown from the iron heart of a psycho-ideo-legal religion. It was formed as a retreat in the 1880s and came fully equipped with laws, ideals, and customs.

—*John Steinbeck*, Sweet Thursday

Suburbs, developments, and intersections, and here we are in Pasadena. Softly sloping avenues loll between orange trees and thickset palms.

—*Simone de Beauvoir*, America Day by Day

The camp that will be named Placerville is earlier called Hangtown.
When a mob forgets to tie the hands of a condemned man and he
clutches the rope above him, someone beats his hands with a pistol
until he lets go.

—*John McPhee*, Assembling California

What I remembered from my childhood here [Reseda], especially a
rural countryside of farms and orchards out toward Canoga Park and
Granada Hills, was not merely "gone." It had been obliterated, as if
by a kind of warfare, and the remnant earth dimmed beneath a
hideous pall of brown air.

—*Barry Lopez*, Replacing Memory

Salinas was never a pretty town. It took a darkness from the
swamps. The high gray fog hung over it and the ceaseless wind
blew up the valley, cold and with a kind of desolate monotony.
The mountains on both sides of the valley were beautiful, but
Salinas was not and we knew it.

    —*John Steinbeck,* Always Something to Do in Salinas

I caught a ride to San Bernardino. It's a railroad town, and I was
going to hop a freight east. But I didn't do it. I ran into a guy in a
poolroom, and begun playing him one ball in the side.

    —*James M. Cain,* The Postman Always Rings Twice

Life in San Diego was sunny and quiet.

                    —*John Dos Passos,* The 42nd Parallel

Santa Monica—a former beach town of funky bungalows and windswept Pacific views that has now become an overbuilt enclave on the westernmost edge of the Los Angeles sprawl.

—*April Smith*, North of Montana

Until after the second war, South Pasadena was bounded by hills and orange groves and the tracks of the Pacific Electric. . . . The world's finest interurban electrical railway system was replaced by the world's greatest gasoline-fired, smog-producing transportation system. The hills where the coyote cried are now peopled.

—*Lawrence Clark Powell*

[Hollister's] claim to fame in 1947 was as a producer of 74 percent of all the garlic consumed in the United States . . . the kind of town that Hollywood showed the world in the film version of East of Eden . . .

—*H. S. Thompson*, Hell's Angels

I knew after twenty-five years in the Napa Valley, we had the
climate, the soil and the grape growing to be the best in the world.

—*vintner Robert Mondavi*

Stockton was a small place among smaller places strung up and
down the Central Valley, and it had no pretensions, as it does now,
of being a big place.

—*Richard Dokey*

As I see it now, our non-Quaker family started out in Whittier with
several strikes against us. When I was a child there, though, I was
unaware of almost everything except being sturdy and happy.

—*M. F. K. Fisher*

San Gabriel is a sleepy old place, with little to interest the ordinary person. A traveler, passing through it, sees nothing to attract his notice as the train pauses at the station, and he finds his gaze wandering off to the north, where it meets the lofty San Gabriel Mountains, a long line of blue-grey, shimmering in the heat of the plains. There is much beautiful scenery around San Gabriel, and wonderful canyons among these mountains.

—*Charles Franklin Carter,*
Stories of the Old Missions of California

Sisterhood means if you happen to be in Burma and I happen to be in San Diego and I'm married to someone who is very jealous and you're married to somebody who is very possessive, if you call me in the middle of the night, I have to come.

—*Maya Angelou*

Santa Barbara is a paradise; Disneyland is a paradise; the U.S. is a paradise. Paradise is just paradise. Mournful, monotonous, and superficial though it may be, it is paradise. There is no other.

—*Jean Baudrillard*

I can promise you that when I go to Sacramento, I will pump up Sacramento.

—*Governor Arnold Schwarzenegger*

Death Valley is neither dead nor a valley.

—*Jerry Bunin, journalist*

I have never been a hindrance, I have never kept the company waiting, neither have my children, and every step I take will be toward California. Give up! I knew what that meant; a shallow grave in the sand.

*—Juliet Brier, on crossing Death Valley, 1849*

I have returned from Death Valley. I walked across that ghastly place and back again.

*—Zane Grey*

The valley we call Death, isn't really that different from much of the rest of the desert West. It's just a little deeper, a little hotter and a little drier. What sets it apart more than anything else is the mind's eye.

*—Richard E. Lingenfelter*

A miner is buried in Rough and Ready. As shovels move, gold appears in his grave. Services continue while mourners stake claims. So goes the story, dust to dust.

—*John McPhee*, Assembling California

One of the things I had a hard time getting used to when I came to California in '78 was Santa Claus in shorts.

—*actor Dennis Franz*

Move to California. Malibu is paradise.

—*businessman David Geffen*

California, Labor Day Weekend . . . early, with ocean fog still in the streets, outlaw motorcyclists wearing shades and greasy Levis roll out from damp garages, all-night diners and cast-off one-night pads in Frisco, Hollywood, Berdoo and East Oakland, heading for the Monterey peninsula, north of Big Sur . . .

*—H. S. Thompson,* Hell's Angels

If you had brain one in that huge melon on top of your neck, you would be living the sweet life out in Southern California's beautiful San Fernando Valley!

*—Dr. Peter Venkman, played by actor*
*Bill Murray, to the demon that terrorizes*
*New York City in* Ghostbusters II

Memphis was almost like going to California. Beale Street was the
black man's street.

—*blues musician Muddy Waters*

For three more mornings she [Susan Ward] awoke in her bare room,
breathing air strangely scented and listening to the strange sounds
that had awakened her: once the bells of the panadero's burro
coming up the trail with loaves sticking out of the panniers on both
sides, twice the distant beating of kettles and hullabaloo of voices
yelling in a strange tongue—the Chinese arising in their camp
under the hill.

—*Wallace Stegner, description of*
*New Almaden in* Angle of Repose

So if you're thinking of moving West
Forget about West L.A.
And forget about
Torrance baby
Cause [sic] Carson girls are A-OK
                    —*lyrics from the song "Carson Girls"*
        *by early '80s L.A. punk band Angry Samoans*

Hi. Welcome to the future: San Dimas, California – 2688. And I'm telling you, it's great here. The air is clean, the water is clean, even the dirt is clean! Bowling averages are way up, minigolf scores are way down. And we have more excellent waterslides than any other planet we communicate with. I'm telling you, this place is great!
                    —*from the movie* Bill and Ted's
                            Excellent Adventure

# VII

# THE REAL
# TINSEL
# UNDERNEATH

Hollywood and the Movies

I'm not very keen on Hollywood. I'd rather have a nice cup of cocoa, really.

—*Noel Coward*

I'm not a little girl from a little town making good in a big town. I'm a big girl from a big town making good in a little town.

—*Mae West arriving in Hollywood*

My fun days are over.

—*James Dean, shortly before his fatal car crash in 1955*

Grace almost always laid the leading man . . . She was famous
for that in this town.

—*Gore Vidal on Grace Kelly*

Who do I fuck to get off this picture?

—*anonymous Hollywood actress, circa 1930*

No wonder the film industry started in the desert in California
where, like all desert dwellers, they dream their buildings, rather
than design them.

—*architect Arthur Erickson*

Every man I've known has fallen in love with Gilda and wakened with me.

> —*Rita Hayworth, referring to her role in the movie* Gilda

Judy [Garland] didn't die of anything, except wearing out. She just plain wore out.

> —*Ray Bolger*

A woman's ass is for her husband, not theatergoers.

> —*Louis B. Mayer*

Put my ashes in a box and tell the messenger to bring them to Louis B. Mayer's office with a farewell message from me. Then when the messenger gets to Louis' desk, I want him to open the box and blow the ashes in the bastard's face.

—*screenwriter and novelist Bud Schulberg*

I'd have liked to have gone to bed with Jean Harlow. She was a beautiful broad. The fellow who married her was impotent and he killed himself. I would have done the same thing.

—*Groucho Marx*

Cocaine isn't habit-forming. I should know—I've been using it for years.

—*Tallulah Bankhead*

I'm going to die young. I just can't stop destroying myself.

*—John Belushi, shortly before his fatal overdose of cocaine and heroin*

He was in California at Paramount when I was, and for six months I ate lunch within 20 feet of him. He always ate alone . . . He was sour, scowling, and ill-humored, as well as a notorious tightwad.

*—James M. Cain on Maurice Chevalier*

There's one thing I want to make clear right off: my baby was a virgin the day she met Errol Flynn.

*—Florence Aadland, about her 15-year-old daughter Beverly's relationship with the Robin Hood star*

John Barrymore was a serious actor who did a great deal of research for all his parts, until, I guess, he was around 50. Then he started drinking heavily . . . So he drank himself to death. It took him 10 years.

—*John Carradine*

I started at the top and worked my way down.

—*Orson Welles*

In California/Beverly Hills, they don't throw away their garbage— they make it into TV shows.

—*Woody Allen*

I wish there was a knob on the TV so you could turn up the intelligence. They got one called "brightness," but it doesn't work, does it?

*—Gallagher, American stand-up comic*

My film is not a movie; it's not about Vietnam. It is Vietnam.

*—Francis Ford Coppla on* Apocalypse Now

That's the trouble with directors. Always biting the hand that lays the golden egg.

*—Sam Goldwyn*

Scarface or something would open, and I would go see the first show, first day. No one could go with me. I didn't want anyone else to ruin it. It was like a religious experience.

—*Quentin Tarantino*

The dumbest question I've ever been asked was, "Why did you leave Milwaukee?" I said, "By 1972, film production had pretty much dried up in Wisconsin!"

—*David Zucker*

Acting is by far and away the toughest job, in terms of film-making and maybe even the arts. How they (the actors) do it I don't know, but they have to be allowed to get their satisfaction.

—*Jonathan Demme*

Women have it harder here (in Hollywood) because there is a lot of money to be made, but men don't like women to have money and power.

—*Penelope Spheeris*

He was macabre. When I was a little girl, he sent me a gift of a replica of my mother [actress Tippi Hedren] in a coffin. That was his idea of a joke. He had a sick sense of humor.

—*Melanie Griffith on Alfred Hitchcock*

Why all the fuss? After all, I just played myself.

—*Errol Flynn, responding to positive reviews for* The Sun Also Rises

I saw the boy in her [Stella Adler's] classrooms, and the genius Stella was talking about was not apparent to the naked eye. He looked to me like a kid who delivers groceries.

—*Clifford Odets on Marlon Brando*

I'll never make another [Andy] Hardy picture . . . I'm fed up with these dopey, insipid parts. How long can a guy play a jerk kid? I'm 27 years old. I've been divorced once and separated from my second wife. I have two boys of my own. I spent almost two years in the army. It's time Judge Hardy went out and bought me a double-breasted suit.

—*Mickey Rooney*

I'm not a real movie star. I've still got the same wife I started out with twenty-eight years ago.

—*Will Rogers*

If you have to have a job in this world, a high-priced movie star is a pretty good gig.

*—Tom Hanks*

I do not regret one professional enemy I have made. Any actor who doesn't dare to make an enemy should get out of the business.

*—Bette Davis*

A star on a movie set is like a time bomb. That bomb has got to be defused so people can approach it without fear.

*—Jack Nicholson*

. . . vacant, vacuous Hollywood was everything I wanted to mould my life into.

—*Andy Warhol*

If my films make one person miserable, I'll feel I have done my job.

—*Woody Allen*

I don't think Hollywood knows any kids, by the time they get here they aren't kids anymore.

—*Dick Clark*

If only those who dream about Hollywood knew how difficult it all is.

—Greta Garbo

This stammer got me a house in Beverly Hills, and I'm not about to screw with it now.

—Bob Newhart

I've always thought of John Travolta as one of the greatest movie stars Hollywood has ever produced.

—Quentin Tarantino

In order to feel safer on his private jet, actor John Travolta has purchased a bomb-sniffing dog. Unfortunately for the actor, the dog came six movies too late.

—*Tina Fey, comedian on* Saturday Night Live

Adam Sandler is a genius performer who writes his own movies and is almost failure-proof. There's something about Adam Sandler that's magical. The rest of us have to work hard.

—*David Zucker*

Don't forget Mother's Day. Or as they call it in Beverly Hills, Dad's Third Wife Day.

—*Jay Leno*

Ever since they found out that Lassie was a boy, the public has believed the worst about Hollywood.

—*Groucho Marx*

Hollywood is like life, you face it with the sum total of your equipment.

—*Joan Crawford*

It was one of history's great love stories, the mutually profitable romance which Hollywood and bohunk America conducted almost in the dark, a tapping of fervent messages through the wall of the San Gabriel Range.

—*John Updike*

Hollywood is a place where they place you under contract instead of under observation.

*—Walter Winchell*

Half the people in Hollywood are dying to be discovered and the other half are afraid they will be.

*—Lionel Barrymore*

The movies are now beyond that peep-show stage when they could be stampeded by every passing fad; they are too dignified to take opportunistic advantage of every cause celebre that comes along.

*—Will Hays*

Hollywood is no place for a woman to find a husband, especially her own.

*—Denise Darcel*


It's not what you are in Hollywood—it's what people think you are.

*—Robert Stack*


The best thing that we can hope for is that the Earth stops spinning, then the Mir spacecraft falls on [actress] Cameron Manheim.

*—Phil Hendrie, comedy radio show host,*
*in the character of General Johnson Jameson*

Hollywood keeps before its child audiences a string of glorified young heroes, everyone of whom is an unhesitating and violent Anarchist. His one answer to everything that annoys him or disparages his country or his parents or his young lady or his personal code of manly conduct is to give the offender a "sock" in the jaw.

—*George Bernard Shaw*

That's what comes of taking vulgarians from the gutter and making idols of them.

—*Kenneth Anger*, Hollywood Babylon

Hollywood's a place where they'll pay you a thousand dollars for a kiss, and fifty cents for your soul. I know, because I turned down the first offer often enough and held out for the fifty cents.

—*Marilyn Monroe*

Hollywood didn't kill Marilyn Monroe, it's the Marilyn Monroes who are killing Hollywood.

*—Billy Wilder*

If my films don't show a profit, I know I'm doing something right.

*—Woody Allen*

There are only three ages for women in Hollywood: Babe, District Attorney, and Driving Miss Daisy.

*—Goldie Hawn, from* The First Wives Club, *by Olivia Goldsmith and Robert Harling*

The only "ism" Hollywood believes in is plagiarism.

*—Dorothy Parker*

Strip away the phony tinsel of Hollywood and you find the real tinsel underneath.

*—Oscar Levant*

You have to be self-reliant and strong to survive in this town. Otherwise you will be destroyed.

*—Joan Crawford*

After two years in Washington, I often long for the realism and sincerity of Hollywood.

—*former Senator Fred Thompson*

You know, OJ was a really nice guy, and he knew his lines. He was nice to everybody on the set. He got to be a better actor, I thought, with every movie.

—*David Zucker*

All Hollywood corrupts; and absolute Hollywood corrupts absolutely.

—*Edmund Wilson*

Hollywood is an extraordinary kind of temporary place.
*—British director John Schlesinger*

Over in Hollywood they almost made a great picture, but they
caught it in time.
*—Wilson Mizner*

In Hollywood a starlet is the name for any woman under thirty
who is not actively employed in a brothel.
*—Ben Hecht*

"Hello," he lied.

*—Don Carpenter quoting a Hollywood agent*

The Hollywood tradition I like best is called "sucking up to the stars."

*—Johnny Carson*

In Hollywood, an equitable divorce settlement means each party getting fifty percent of publicity.

*—Lauren Bacall*

You can take all the sincerity in Hollywood, place it in the navel of a fruit fly and still have room enough for three caraway seeds and a producer's heart.

—*Fred Allen*

Hollywood is like being nowhere and talking to nobody about nothing.

—*Michelangelo Antonioni*

They've great respect for the dead in Hollywood, but none for the living.

—*Errol Flynn*

In Hollywood gratitude is Public Enemy Number One.

—*Hedda Hopper*

[Making movies) is the kissiest business in the world. You have to keep kissing people when you're penned up and working together the way we are. If people making a movie didn't keep kissing, they'd be at each other's throats.

—*Ava Gardner*

Hollywood is a place where a man can get stabbed in the back while climbing a ladder.

—*William Faulkner*

At night thousands of names and slogans are outlined in neon, and searchlight beams often pierce the sky, perhaps announcing a motion picture premiere, perhaps the opening of a new hamburger stand.

—*from* California: A Guide To The Golden State

Hollywood is a place where people from Iowa mistake each other for a star.

—*Fred Allen*

In Hollywood, if you don't have happiness you send out for it.

—*Rex Reed*

You'll never know how dull this town is until you move here with your wife and kids.

—*screenwriter Martin Ragaway*

When I was growing up in Watts, I would listen to Nat 'King' Cole and I'd look at that purple Capitol logo . . . and later I'd walk from Dorsey High School all the way up to Hollywood just to look at the Capitol Building.

—*Arthur Lee, member of the rock band Love*

The most beautiful slave quarters in the world.

—*Moss Hart*

Hollywood is a world with all the personality of a paper cup.

—*Raymond Chandler*

Hollywood [is] a place where you spend more than you make on things you don't need to impress people you don't like.

—*comedian Ken Murray*

Living in Hollywood is like living in a lit cigar butt.

—*Phyllis Diller*

If we have to kiss Hollywood good-bye, it may be with one of those tender, old-fashioned, seven-second kisses as exchanged between two people of the opposite sex with all their clothes on.

—*Anita Loos*

Millions are to be grabbed out here and your only competition is idiots. Don't let this get around.

—*Herman Mankiewicz telling Ben Hecht about Hollywood*

Hollywood impresses me as being ten million dollars worth of intricate and high ingenious machinery functioning elaborately to put skin on baloney.

—*George Jean Nathan*

[Hollywood is] A trip through a sewer in a glass-bottomed boat.

—*Wilson Mizner*

[Hollywood is] a great place to live, but I wouldn't want to visit there.

—*Will Rogers*

Hollywood money isn't money. It's congealed snow, melts in your hand and there you are.

—*Dorothy Parker*

We don't want any poor Englishmen hanging around Hollywood.
                    —*Evelyn Waugh*, The Loved One

The head boy at Harrow survived the war to become an English butler in Hollywood, a profession for which his education had prepared him admirably.
                              —*John Mortimer*

Everybody in Hollywood knows his business, plus music.
                    —*composer Alfred E. Newman*

For some guys/The dream is Paris.
But I found a shrine/Where Hollywood Boulevard crosses Vine.

—*Ervin Drake, "My Hometown"*

I came out here with one suit and everybody said I looked like a bum. Twenty years later Marlon Brando came out with only a sweatshirt and the town drooled over him. That shows how much Hollywood has progressed.

—*Humphrey Bogart*

The only reason I'm in Hollywood is that I don't have the moral courage to refuse the money.

—*Marlon Brando*

I regret the passing of the studio system. I was very appreciative of it because I had no talent.

—*Lucille Ball*

If you have a vagina and an attitude in this town, then that's a lethal combination.

—*Sharon Stone*

If my books had been any worse, I should not have been invited to Hollywood, and . . . if they had been any better, I should not have come.

—*Raymond Chandler*

To survive there, you need the ambition of a Latin-American revolutionary, the ego of a grand opera tenor, and the physical stamina of a cow pony.

—*Billie Burke*

You can take Hollywood for granted like I did, or you can dismiss it with the contempt we reserve for what we don't understand. It can be understood too, but only dimly and in flashes. Not half a dozen men have ever been able to keep the whole equation of pictures in their heads.

—*F. Scott Fitzgerald*, The Last Tycoon

By provision of concert halls, modern libraries, theatres and suitable centres we desire to assure our people full access to the great heritage of culture in this nation. How satisfactory it would be if different parts of the citizenry would again walk their several ways as they once did. Let every part of merrie England be merry in its own way. Death to Hollywood!

—*John Maynard Keynes*

Hollywood's like Egypt, full of crumbled pyramids. It'll never come back. It'll just keep on crumbling until finally the wind blows the last studio prop across the sands.

—*producer David O. Selznick*

Longe de Deus e perto de Hollywood. [So far from God and so
near to Hollywood.]

—*Paulo Antonio Paranaguá,*
*subtitle of his history of Latin American cinema*

This place [Hollywood] is tricky because it operates with optimism.
If you get a "yes" it means "maybe"; if you get a "maybe" I'm afraid it
tends to mean "no"; and if you get a "no" you might as well pack up
and go home.

—*British film director Michael Tuchner*

Hollywood is interested in power, not money. People who are
interested in money do not go into the film business.

—*Orson Welles*

The motion picture made in Hollywood, if it is to create art at all, must do so within such strangling limitations of subject and treatment that it is a blind wonder it ever achieves any distinction beyond the purely mechanical slickness of a glass and chrome bathroom.

*—Raymond Chandler*

You don't resign from these jobs, you escape from them.

*—Dawn Steel, on leaving the presidency of Columbia Pictures*

We are the top nation and we need history to explain how we got here. If that means stealing your history and heroes to do it, then Hollywood will think it's a small price to pay for success at the box office.

*—Sherl Bearlstrom, author of* Hollywood and History

Hollywood is a carnival where there are no concessions.

*—Wilson Mizener*

The Garden of Allah apartments is the sort of place you expect to find down the rabbit hole.

*—Alexander Woollcott*

That was my one big Hollywood hit, but, in a way, it hurt my picture career. After that, I was typecast as a lion, and there just weren't many parts for lions.

*—Bert Lahr, referring to his role as the Cowardly Lion in* The Wizard of Oz

I was living at the Garden of Allah as a merry bachelor when Ross
arrived from the East. I was awakened at a very early hour by the
sound of his shaking a dice box outside my window. He was all
ready to play, with a backgammon board . . . We had quite a long
session, and every hour or so he would bellow, "Where are all those
Hollywood beauties I've heard so much about?"

Unbeknownst to him, I finally arranged with the local madam
to send over three of her more presentables. But when they arrived,
he furiously handed each girl twenty bucks and said, "Go home,
girls, I'm on a triple blitz!"

—*Harpo Marx on* The New Yorker *editor Harold Ross*

People's sex habits are as well known in Hollywood as their
political opinions, and much less criticized.

—*Ben Hecht*

I believe that God felt sorry for actors so he created Hollywood to give them a place in the sun and a swimming pool. The price they had to pay was to surrender their talent.

—*Sir Cedric Hartwick*

This is a terrible confession to make, but after I left the Army I had a number of things to try. I had a great conceit to think that if all else failed I could always go to Hollywood. So when all else did fail I really went to Hollywood. And then I found out how wrong I was.

—*David Niven*

I always thought the real violence in Hollywood isn't what's on the screen. It's what you have to do to raise the money.

—*David Mamet*

Bankers, nepotists, contracts and talkies: on four fingers one may count the leeches which have sucked a young and vigorous industry into paresis.

*—screenwriter Dalton Trumbo*

Hollywood, to hear some writers tell it, is the place where they take an author's steak tartare and make cheeseburger out of it. Upon seeing the film, they say, the author promptly cuts his throat, bleeding to death in a pool of money.

*—author Fletcher Knebel*

It goes back to all of us wanting to be in Hollywood. We're all dying to win an Oscar.

*—Jerry Della Famina*

The overall picture, as the boys say, is of a degraded community whose idealism even is largely fake. The pretentiousness, the bogus enthusiasm, the constant drinking and drabbing, the incessant squabbling over money, the all-pervasive agent, the strutting of the big shots . . . the constant fear of losing all this fairy gold and being the nothing they have never ceased to be, the snide tricks, the whole damn mess is out of this world.

—*Raymond Chandler*

We Americans have always considered Hollywood, at best, a sinkhole of depraved venality. And, of course, it is. It is not a Protective Monastery of Aesthetic Truth. It is a place where everything is incredibly expensive.

—*David Mamet*

How did I get to Hollywood? By train.

*—director John Ford*

Hollywood has always been a cage . . . a cage to catch our dreams.

*—director John Houston*

Pearl is a disease of oysters. Levant is a disease of Hollywood.

*—critic Kenneth Tynan on wit and pianist Oscar Levant*

I think any girl who comes to Hollywood with sex symbol or bombshell hanging over her has a rough road ahead.

*—Kim Basinger*

How could a New Yorker possibly take something called the
Hollywood String Quartet seriously?

—*Leonard Slatkin*

I attribute [success] to having the background of just loving the
great stories of the world—and that's what makes the most successful films—combined with my trashy, vulgar appreciation of all that
is modern Hollywood.

—*Leslie Dixon*

It's said in Hollywood that you should always forgive your
enemies—because you never know when you'll have to work
with them.

—*Lana Turner*

[Hollywood is] a mining town in lotus land.

—*F. Scott Fitzgerald*

Cary Grant, born Archie Leach, was a poor boy who could barely spell posh. That's acting for you—or maybe Hollywood.

—*Melvin Maddocks*

Hollywood is the only industry, even taking in soup companies, which does not have laboratories for the purpose of experimentation.

—*Orson Welles*

In Hollywood, all marriages are happy. It's trying to live together afterwards that causes the problems.

—*Shelly Winters*

No one has a closest friend in Hollywood.

—*Sheila Graham*

When I was very young and first worked in Hollywood, the films had bred in me one sole ambition: to get away from them; to live in the great world outside movies; to meet people who created their own situations through living them; who ad-libbed their own dialogue; whose jokes were not the contrivance of some gag writer.

—*Anita Loos*

Suicide is much easier and more acceptable in Hollywood than growing old gracefully.

—*Julie Burchill*

I don't want to see pictures of Hollywood stars in their dressing gowns taking out the rubbish. It ruins the fantasy.

—*Sarah Brightman*

I was like a kept woman during my twenty-one years at MGM. Hollywood was like an expensive, beautifully run club. You didn't need to carry money. Your face was your credit card—all over the world.

—*actor Walter Pidgeon*

My driving abilities from Mexico have helped me get through Hollywood.

—*Salma Hayek*

Hollywood grew to be the most flourishing factory of popular mythology since the Greeks.

—*Alistair Cooke*

It's somehow symbolic of Hollywood that Tara was just a facade, with no rooms inside.

—*producer David O. Selznick*

Hollywood is more forgiving than the church.

—*Richard Rossi*

Hollywood amuses me. Holier-than-thou for the public and unholier-than-the-devil in reality.

—*Grace Kelly*

Where is Hollywood located? Chiefly between the ears. In that part of the American brain lately vacated by God.

—*Erica Jong*

In Hollywood, brides keep the bouquets and throw away the groom.

—*Groucho Marx*

Just like those other black holes from outer space, Hollywood is postmodern to this extent: it has no center, only a spreading dead zone of exhaustion, inertia, and brilliant decay.

—*sociologist Arthur Kroker*

I have been asked if I ever get the DTs; I don't know; it's hard to tell where Hollywood ends and the DTs begin.

—*W. C. Fields*

In Hollywood now when people die they don't say, Did he leave a will? but Did he leave a diary?

—*Liza Minelli*

Hollywood makes prostitutes out of women and sissies out of men.

—*source unknown*

Hollywood died on me as soon as I got there.

—*Orson Welles*

The bite of existence did not cut into one in Hollywood . . .
—*Mae West*

Hollywood always wanted me to be pretty, but I fought for realism.
—*Bette Davis*

Every country gets the circus it deserves. Spain gets bullfights. Italy gets the Catholic Church. America gets Hollywood.
—*Erica Jong*

I can't talk about Hollywood. It was a horror to me when I was there and it's a horror to look back on. I can't imagine how I did it. When I got away from it I couldn't even refer to the place by name. "Out there," I called it.

—*Dorothy Parker*

In Hollywood, the women are all peaches. It makes one long for an apple occasionally.

—*W. Somerset Maugham*

They'll always be an England, even if it's in Hollywood.

—*Bob Hope*

There is in Hollywood, as in all cultures in which gambling is the central activity, a lowered sexual energy, an inability to devote more than token attention to the preoccupations of the society outside. The action is everything, more consuming than sex, more immediate than politics; more important always than the acquisition of money, which is never, for the gambler, the true point of the exercise.

*—Joan Didion*

Some say, what is the salvation of the movies? I say run 'em backwards. It can't hurt 'em and it's worth a trial.

*—Will Rogers*

A wide screen just makes a bad film twice as bad.

*—Sam Goldwyn*

The average Hollywood film star's ambition is to be admired by an American, courted by an Italian, married to an Englishman and have a French boyfriend.

—*Katharine Hepburn*

Working in Hollywood does give one a certain expertise in the field of prostitution.

—*Jane Fonda*

There's so few people in this town with a conscience.

—*director Blake Edwards*

At the Academy Award Dinners all the actors and actresses in
Hollywood gather around to see what someone else thinks about
their acting besides their press agents.

—*Bob Hope*

Much more frequent in Hollywood than the emergence of
Cinderella is her sudden vanishing. At our party, even in those
glowing days, the clock was always striking twelve for someone at
the height of greatness; and there was never a prince to fetch her
back to the happy scene.

—*Ben Hecht*

Hollywood gives a young girl the aura of one giant, self-contained orgy farm, its inhabitants dedicated to crawling into every pair of pants they can find.

—*Veronica Lake*

If God doesn't destroy Hollywood Boulevard, he owes Sodom and Gomorrah an apology.

—*Jay Leno*

In the past, as now, [Hollywood] was a stamping ground for taste-lessness, violence, and hyperbole, but once upon a time it turned out a product which sweetened the flavor of life all over the world.

—*Anita Loos*

Hollywood is the worst of the dope peddlers because it sells its opium under a false label. Its customers pull at the pipe in the belief that it is harmless and, when they finally give it up, find that they are still helplessly dreaming the former delusions.

*—George Jean Nathan*

Never in my life have I seen so many unhappy men making a hundred thousand dollars a year.

*—Nick Schenck, studio head during the '30s and '40s*

In case of air raid, go directly to RKO—they haven't had a hit in years.

*—source unknown, during World War II*

Go see that turkey for yourself, and see for yourself why you shouldn't see it.

—*Sam Goldwyn*

What's the matter?—don't you serve servicemen?

—*actor Jim Bachus, wearing a Roman centurion costume during the filming of* Demetrius and the Gladiators, *to an incredulous bartender*

Movie actors wear dark glasses to funerals to conceal the fact that their eyes are not red from weeping.

—*scriptwriter Nunnally Johnson*

If you must get in trouble, do it at the Chateau Marmont
[a legendary Hollywood hotel].

> —*Columbia Pictures head Harry Cohn*
> *to William Holden and Glenn Ford*

The end of Hollywood was always predictable. There were always
financial crises. Someone would come out from the East, and
announce that the business was in deep trouble, and, literally, what
would happen was that they'd reduce the number of matzo balls in
Louie Mayer's chicken soup at the commissary from three to two in
each portion.

> —*Joseph L. Mankiewicz*

My attitude about Hollywood is that I wouldn't walk across the street to pull one of those executives out of the snow if he was bleeding to death. Not unless I was paid for it. None of them ever did me any favors.

—*James Woods*

[Hollywood] is filled with people who make adventure pictures and who have never left this place . . . religious pictures and they haven't been in a church or synagogue for years . . . pictures about love and they have never been in love—ever.

—*Richard Brooks*

The people here [in Hollywood] seem to live in a little world that shuts out the rest of the universe and everyone appears to be faking life. The actors and writers live in fear, and nothing, including the houses, seems permanent.

*—Fred Allen*

. . . as she moved from table to table, endeavoring to understand the [gambling] games, she realized that either her memory was at fault or Hollywood had carelessly added an apocryphal glitter and subtracted an essential gloom.

*—Jean Stafford*

[In Hollywood] they know only one word of more than one syllable, and that is "fill-um."

—*Louis Sherwin*

Orson [Welles] is not a man who could bow down to idiots. And Hollywood is full of them. Orson has a big ego—but he's completely logical. He is a joy! An amateur—I mean that in the very best sense of the word. He loves pictures and plays and all things theatrical.

—*John Huston*

Personally, I'm not much of a one for Hollywood parties. I like my work and when I'm done, I like to enjoy the privacy in my house with my wife and daughter. To me, being at home with them is glamorous.

—*Antonio Banderas*

No one "goes Hollywood"—they were that way before they came here. Hollywood just exposed it.

—*Ronald Reagan*

I went out there [Hollywood] for a thousand a week, and I worked Monday, and I got fired Wednesday. The guy that hired me was out of town Tuesday.

—*Nelson Algren*

[Hollywood's] idea of "production value" is spending a million dollars dressing up a story that any good writer would throw away. Its vision of the rewarding movie is a vehicle for some glamour-puss with two expressions and eighteen changes of costume, or for some male idol of the muddled millions with a permanent hangover, six worn-out acting tricks, the build of a lifeguard, and the mentality of a chicken-strangler.

—*Raymond Chandler*

Hollywood is where they shoot too many pictures and not enough actors.

—*Walter Winchell*

Hollywood is like Picasso's bathroom.

—*Candice Bergen*

The convictions of Hollywood and television are made of boiled money.

—*Lillian Hellman*

I discovered early in my movie work that a movie is never any better than the stupidest man connected with it. There are times when this distinction may be given to the writer or director. Most often it belongs to the producer.

—*Ben Hecht*

Hollywood is bounded on the north, south, east and west by agents.

—*William Fadiman*

Hollywood—that's where they give Academy awards to Charlton Heston for acting.

—*Shirley Knight*

The people are unreal. The flowers are unreal, they don't smell. The food is unreal, it doesn't taste of anything. The whole place is a glaring, gaudy, nightmarish set, built up in the desert.

—*Ethel Barrymore*

You can't find any true closeness in Hollywood, because everybody does the fake closeness so well.

—*Carrie Fisher*

In Hollywood the woods are full of people that learned to write but evidently can't read; if they could read their stuff, they'd stop writing.

—*Will Rogers*

Hollywood is loneliness beside the swimming pool.

—*Liv Ullman*

A dreary industrial town controlled by hoodlums of enormous wealth, the ethical sense of a pack of jackals, and taste so degraded that it befouled everything to touch it.

—*S. J. Perelman*

[Hollywood] always sounds glamorous when you're young.

—*Patricia Neal*

I am not interested in money. I just want to be wonderful.

—*Marilyn Monroe*

What I like about Hollywood is that one can get along quite well by knowing two words of English—swell and lousy.

—*Vicki Baum*

[Hollywood's] beauty standard is so strict. Even though I may not be their ideal, it doesn't mess me up. I feel like some of those money guys are the guys from my high school who didn't find me attractive.

—*Elizabeth Taylor*

I'm a Hollywood writer, so I put on my sports jacket and take off my brain.

—*Ben Hecht*

Isn't Hollywood a dump—in the human sense of the word. A hideous town, pointed up by the insulting gardens of its rich, full of the human spirit at a new low of debasement.

—*F. Scott Fitzgerald*

Hollywood isn't your cesspool, America. It's your mirror.

—*Bill Maher*

I think there is a predisposition among Christians that Hollywood is anti-Jesus or anti-Christianity. I was warned I'd have to fight to maintain the freedom to express my beliefs. It's an unfair stereotype, and so far that's been the farthest from the truth.

—*Clay Aiken*

Failure is regarded in Hollywood as practically a contagious disease; people will literally cross the road to avoid someone who is tainted with it.

—*Barry Norman*, The Film Greats

In Hollywood the man who cleans your pool is an actor. The man who sells you your copy of Variety is an actor. I don't think there's a real person left in the place.

—*Neil Gaiman*

Today, the only thing Hollywood swears by is space adventures because that's what goes over well. For my part, I trust my instinct and I make the films I believe in. If the public follows me, that's wonderful. If it doesn't follow, "c'est la vie."

*—Clint Eastwood*

In Hollywood a girl's virtue is much less important than her hairdo.

*—Marilyn Monroe*

The way to be successful in Hollywood is to be as obnoxious as the next guy.

*—Sylvester Stallone*

Goethe said, "Talent is developed in privacy," you know? And it's really true. There is a need for aloneness which I don't think most people realize for an actor. It's almost having certain kinds of secrets for yourself that you'll let the whole world in on only for a moment, when you're acting.

—*Marilyn Monroe*

Everybody steals from everybody, that's Hollywood.

—*Jon Favreau*

Hollywood is a place that attracts people with massive holes in their souls.

—*Julia Phillips*

There's nothing the matter with Hollywood that a good earthquake couldn't cure.

—*Moss Hart*

The most expensive habit in the world is celluloid, not heroin, and I need a fix every few years.

—*Steven Spielberg*

You can fool all the people all the time if the advertising is right and the budget is big enough.

—*Joseph E. Levine*

Hosting the Oscars is like making love to a beautiful woman—it's something I only get to do when Billy Crystal's out of town.
                              —*Steve Martin, at the 2001 Academy Awards*

They used to shoot her through gauze. You should shoot me through linoleum.
                              —*Tallulah Bankhead, referring to Shirley Temple*

An associate producer is the only guy in Hollywood who will associate with a producer.
                                                          —*Fred Allen*

All Americans born between 1890 and 1945 wanted to be
movie stars.

*—Gore Vidal*

Give me a couple of years, and I'll make that actress an overnight
success.

*—Sam Goldwyn*

Talk low, talk slow, and don't say too much.

*—John Wayne*

Out in Hollywood, where the streets are paved with Goldwyn, the word "sophisticate" means, very simply, "obscene." A sophisticated story is a dirty story.

—*Dorothy Parker*

Scriptwriting is the toughest part of the whole racket, the least understood and the least noticed.

—*Frank Capra*

You wanna be a success in this town, kid? Just remember one thing. No one gives a shit about the script.

—*screenwriter Landyn Parker*

You can't do it that way, you'll spoil the anticlimax.
>  —*Michael Curtis, director, to a writer rewriting a scene.*

We movie stars all end up by ourselves. Who knows? Maybe we want to.
>  —*Bette Davis*

What [the critics] call dirty in our pictures, they call lusty in foreign films.
>  —*Bill Wilder*

Hollywood's like Egypt. Full of crumbling pyramids. It'll never come back. It'll just keep on crumbling until finally the wind blows the last studio prop across the sands.

—*Attributed to David Selznick*

I've got America's best writer for $300 a week.

—*Jack Warner, on signing William Faulkner to a script-writing deal*

Everyone's just laughing at me. I hate it. Big breasts, big ass, big deal. Can't I be anything else?

—*Marilyn Monroe*

What are the two biggest reasons for Jane Russell's success?
　　　　　*—Slogan for* The Outlaw, *starring Jane Russell.*
*Anecdotal evidence claims that the underwire bra she wore*
*was designed by producer Howard Hughes, although the*
*actress claims she didn't wear it in the film*

[Howard] Hughes was the only man I ever knew who had to die to prove he had been alive.

　　　　　　　　　　　　　*—Walter Kane*

Who the hell wants to hear actors talk?
　　　　　　　　*—movie producer Harry M. Warner*

Our Boeing 747 has been fleeing westward from darkened California, racing across the Pacific toward the sun, the incandescent eye of God, but slowly, three hours later than West Coast time, twilight gathers outside, veil upon lilac veil.

—*William Manchester*

I don't care if it doesn't make a nickel. I just want every man, woman, and child in America to see it.

—*Sam Goldwyn*

They scowled at dialogue, shuddered at jokes, and wrestled with a script until they had shaken out of it all the verbal glitter and bright plotting. Thus they were able to bring to the screen evidence only of their own "genius."

—*Ben Hecht on working with some directors*

Being a screenwriter in Hollywood is like being a eunuch at an orgy. Worse, actually, at least the eunuch is allowed to watch.

*—Albert Brooks*

Studio executives are intelligent, brutally overworked men and women who share one thing in common with baseball managers: they wake up every morning of the world with the knowledge that sooner or later they're going to get fired.

*—William Goldman*

A good film is when the price of the dinner, the theatre admission and the babysitter were worth it.

*—Alfred Hitchcock*

They have followed their usual procedure and handed my treatment over to several other people to make a screenplay out of it. By the time they are ready to shoot it may have been through 20 pairs of hands. What will be left? One shudders to think. Meanwhile, they have paid me a lot of money.

—*Aldous Huxley*

They told me to fix my teeth, change my nose, even get out of the business. But I stayed and learned and didn't give up.

—*Lauren Hutton*

The movies are the only court where the judge goes to the lawyer for advice.

—*F. Scott Fitzgerald*

Wet she was a star—dry she ain't.
> —*studio head Joe Pasternak on swimmer*
> *Esther William's film career*

If I make a good movie they say I'm a British director and if I make what they think is a bad one, they say I'm Irish!
> —*Neil Jordan*

We have that Indian scene. We can get the Indians from the reservoir.
> —*Sam Goldwyn*

The lunatics have taken charge of the asylum.
—*Richard Roland, referring to the creation of United Artists studio by director D.W. Griffin and actors Charlie Chaplin, Douglas Fairbanks, and Mary Pickford*

Any idiot can get laid when they're famous. That's easy. It's getting laid when you're not famous that takes some talent.
—*Kevin Bacon*

The words "Kiss Kiss Bang Bang," which I saw on an Italian movie poster, are perhaps the briefest statement imaginable on the basic appeal of movies.
—*Pauline Kael*

I'm no actor. And I have sixty-four pictures to prove it.

—*Victor Mature*

I am not a celebrity. I am a human being.

—*Landyn Parker, screenwriter*

You call this a script? Give me a couple of $5,000-a-week writers and I'll write it myself.

—*Joe Pasternak, producer*

I'll do anything for money—even associate with my agent.

—*Vincent Price*

The movie owners are the only troupe in the history of entertainment that has never been seduced by the adventure of the entertainment world.

—*Ben Hecht*

Movies have just become a kind of hallucination. An excuse to hallucinate, like drugs. Movies are a dream world. Eat popcorn and dream.

—*Sam Shephard*

MGM bores me when I see them, but I don't see them much. They have been a help in getting me introductions to morticians, who are the only people worth knowing.

—*Evelyn Waugh*

The director is the most overrated artist in the world. He is the only artist who, with no talent whatsoever, can be a success for 50 years without his lack of talent ever being discovered.

—*Orson Welles*

The trouble with this business is the dearth of bad pictures.

—*Sam Goldwyn*

Keep it out of focus—I want to win the foreign picture award.
> —*Billy Wilder to his cinematographer*
> *shooting* Sunset Boulevard

If you want art, don't mess about with movies. Buy a Picasso.
> —*Michael Winner*

That the film turned out to be coherent is a miracle. That it is successful proves there is a God.
> —*Martin Brest, on directing* Beverly Hills Cop

Do you have any idea how bad the picture is? I'll tell you. Stay away from the neighborhood where it's playing—don't even go near that street! It might rain—you could get caught in the downpour, and to keep dry you'd have to go into the theater.

—*producer Herman Mankiewicz*

Too many Broadway actors in motion pictures lost their grip on success—had a feeling that none of it had ever happened on that sun-drenched coast, that the coast itself did not exist, there was no California.

—*Mae West*

If you're the type of person who has to fulfill your dreams,
you've gotta be resourceful to make sure you can do it. I came out
to California when I was twenty-one, thinking my New York
credentials would take me all the way. I came back home a year
later all dejected and a failure.

*—actor Vin Diesel*

Frank was so completely hip that he went down to Hollywood and
bought the blue and yellow striped sweatshirt that Lee Marvin wore
in The Wild One.

*—H.S. Thompson, on a former president of
the Hell's Angels outlaw motorcycle club,* Hell's Angels

If you're a kid in Southern California, somebody—whether it's you or your parents—somebody throws your hat into the ring and I think everyone had a commercial or two.

*—Danny Bonaduce of* The Partridge Family

~~~

We liked America in spite of everything. Europe was so old, so burdened with guilt complexes. California was a center for mass art. Europe to an artist after the war was not at all interesting. I had become a complete foreigner in Germany. And there, in Hollywood, was an industry for a new art.

*—German director Douglas Sirk*

~~~

I will forgive Pamela [Sue Anderson], and I will go to California, with my friend Mr. Jesus, AND WE WILL TAKE HER!
—*Borat, played by Sasha Baron Cohen,*
*in the movie* Borat

Pamela! I am not attracted to you any more . . . . NOT!
—*Borat, played by Sasha Baron Cohen*

Tom Cruise and Nicole Kidman say their split is amicable, and they want everyone to know that after the divorce is final, their two adopted children will be returned to the prop department at Universal Studios.
—*Tina Fey, comedian on* Saturday Night Live

I want to make a picture about the Russian secret police—the GOP.
                                                    —*Sam Goldwyn*

I found out that Hollywood is more crooked, dumber, crueler,
stupider than all the books I've read about it.
    —*L.A. poet Charles Bukowski, often mistakenly associated with
                                        the Beat Generation*

I don't make films for children. I make films that children aren't
embarrassed to take their parents to.
                                                    —*Walt Disney*

Despite what Walt Disney animated films have taught us, someone is NOT more likely to be a "good" person if they are beautiful (or at least cuddly) or more likely to be "bad" if they are ugly. In fact, it is probably the OPPOSITE of reality. Ironically, the best proof of this comes FROM the behavior of the residents of Hollywood themselves.

—*John Zeigler, L.A. radio talk show host*

There aren't any of these goddam actors that are better than me. None of them. Nobody. Not DeNiro, not Brando, not Jack, not anybody. I have the goods. They have the material.

—*Don Johnson*

My movies were the kind they show in prisons and airplanes, because nobody can leave.

—*Burt Reynolds*

I don't lecture and I don't grind any axes. I just want to entertain.
—*Gregory Peck*

I never watch television because it's an ugly piece of furniture, gives off a hideous light, and, besides, I'm against free entertainment.
—*John Waters, director*

In France, I'm an auteur. In England, I'm a horror movie director. In Germany, I'm a film maker. In the US, I'm a bum.
—*John Carpenter, director*

You can't see California without Marlon Brando's eyes!
—*"Eyeless," lyrics by the metal group Slipknot*

Critics can be your most important friend. I don't read criticism of my stuff only because when it's bad, it's rough—and when it's good, it's not good enough.
—*Kevin Bacon*

I'm English. Our dentistry is not world famous. But I made sure I got moldings of my old teeth beforehand because I miss them.
—*actor Christian Bale*

Let's bring it up to date with some snappy nineteenth century dialogue.

—*Sam Goldwyn*

⌒

These were the hills [outside Hollywood] that the Lone Ranger and Zorro and Roy Rogers and the Cisco Kid used to ride around on in the TV shows of the 1950s. I had never noticed until now that the West of the movies and the West of television were two quite different places. Movie crews had obviously gone out into the real West—the West of buttes and bluffs and red river valleys—while television companies, being cheap, had only just driven a few miles into the hills north of Hollywood and filmed on the edges of orange groves.

—*Bill Bryson*, The Lost Continent

⌒

# VIII

# TWELVE VALLEY GIRLS STUCK ON AN ESCALATOR

*Jokes about California*

## You Know You're In California When . . .

↫ The fastest part of your commute is down your driveway.

↫ You were born somewhere else.

↫ You know how to eat an artichoke.

↫ The primary bugs that you worry about are electronic.

↫ Your car has bulletproof windows.

↫ Left is right and right is wrong.

↫ Your monthly house payments exceed your annual income.

⌒ Your mouse has only one ball.

⌒ You need a new TV, you can run down to the local riot and pick one up.

⌒ You dive under a desk whenever a large truck goes by.

⌒ You can't find your other earring because your son is wearing it.

⌒ You drive to your neighborhood block party.

⌒ Your family tree contains "significant others."

⌒ Your cat has it's own psychiatrist.

⌒ You don't exterminate your roaches, you smoke them.

∽ You see 25 lawyers chasing an ambulance.

∽ More than clothes come out of the closets.

∽ You go to a tanning salon before going to the beach.

∽ Your blind date turns out to be your ex-spouse.

∽ More money is spent on facelifts than on diapers.

∽ When you can't schedule a meeting because you must "do lunch."

∽ Your children learn to walk in Birkenstocks.

∽ Rainstorms or thunder are the lead story for the local news.

- You'll reluctantly miss yoga class to wait for the hot tub repairman.

- You consult your horoscope before planning your day.

- A glass has been reserved for you at your favorite winery.

- When all highways into the state say: "no fruits."

- All highways out of the state say: "Go back."

- You pack shorts and a T-shirt for skiing in the snow, and a sweater and a wetsuit for the beach.

- Your coworker has eight body piercings and none are visible.

➣ You make over $1,000,000 and still can't afford a house.

➣ You take a bus and are shocked at two people carrying on a conversation in English.

➣ Your child's 3rd-grade teacher has purple hair, a nose ring, and is named Flower.

➣ You can't remember . . . is pot illegal?

➣ You've been to a baby shower that has two mothers and a sperm donor.

➣ You have a very strong opinion about where your coffee beans are grown, and you can taste the difference between Sumatran and Ethiopian.

➣ You can't remember . . . is pot illegal?

⤳ A really great parking space can totally move you to tears.

⤳ Gas costs $1.00 per gallon more than anywhere else in the U.S.

⤳ Unlike back home, the guy at 8:30 AM at Starbucks wearing a baseball cap and sunglasses who looks like George Clooney really IS George Clooney.

⤳ Your car insurance costs as much as your house payment.

⤳ You can't remember . . . is pot illegal?

⤳ It's barely sprinkling rain and there's a report on every news station: "STORM WATCH."

⤳ You pass an elementary school playground and the children are all busy with their cells or pagers.

⌒ It's barely sprinkling rain outside, so you leave for work an hour early to avoid all the weather-related accidents.

⌒ HEY!!!! Is pot illegal???

⌒ Both you AND your dog have therapists.

⌒ The Terminator is your governor.

⌒ If you drive illegally, they take your driver's license. If you're here illegally, they want to give you one.

# HOW TO TELL YOU'RE IN SOUTHERN CALIFORNIA

○ A low-speed police pursuit will interrupt ANY TV broadcast.

○ You assume every company offers domestic partner benefits, a fab exercise facility, and tofu takeout.

○ You're thinking of taking an adult class but you can't decide between aromatherapy and conversational Mandarin.

○ Your best friends just named their twins after her acting coach and his personal trainer.

○ The three-hour traffic jam you just sat through wasn't caused by a horrific nine car pile-up, but by everyone slowing to rubberneck at a lost shoe lying on the shoulder.

Why does New Jersey have all the toxic waste dumps and California have all the lawyers?
Because New Jersey got first pick.

A California men's prison hopes to keep inmates from returning to crime by training them for undersea construction and dam. The marine technology training program is taught to prisoners serving 14 months to 4 years sentences. Ironically, the California Institution for Men is landlocked and located on a stretch of former farmland some 40 miles east of Los Angeles.

Did you hear about the near-tragedy at the mall? There was a power outage, and twelve California Valley Girls were stuck on the escalators for over four hours.

You know, I don't know if you know, but in California a man was
just given 25 years to life, for cheating on a DMV test.
                              *—Peter Camejo of the Green Party*

Hell, if KY jelly went off the market, the whole California Angels
pitching staff would be out of baseball.
                    *—former Red Sox pitcher Bill "The Spaceman" Lee*

In California, 50 women protested the impending war with Iraq by
lying on the ground naked and spelling out the word peace. Right
idea, wrong president.

                                              *—Jay Leno*

All creative people should be required to leave California for three months every year.

—*Gloria Swanson*

California is like a bowl of granola; full of fruits, nuts, and flakes.

—*Leo Gallagher*

We all have our little faults. Mine's in California.

—*Lex Luthor,* Superman

I'm a child of southern California. I can't go out in this [rain], I'll melt.

—*Seth, played by actor Adam Brody, from the TV show* The O.C.

[Yosemite] is incredibly, mouth-gawpingly beautiful. Your first view of the El Capitan valley, with its towering mountains and white waterfalls spilling hundreds of feet down to the meadows of the valley floor, makes you think that surely you have expired and gone to heaven. But then you drive down into Yosemite village and realize that if this is heaven you are going to spend the rest of eternity with an awful lot of fat people in Bermuda shorts.

*—Bill Bryson*, The Lost Continent

## THE GOVERNATOR

An old interview of Arnold Schwarzenegger has surfaced where he admits to smoking a lot of pot and having sex with hookers. Finally a Republican all Californians can get behind.

*—David Letterman*

Arnold Schwarzenegger's publicist told USA Today that the actor has not ruled out running for governor of California, saying that he will make a decision soon. Reportedly Arnold needs the time to learn how to pronounce "gubernatorial."

—*comedian Jimmy Fallon*

Earlier today, Arnold Schwarzenegger criticized the California school system, calling it disastrous. Arnold says, "California's schools are so bad that its graduates are willing to vote for me."

—*Conan O'Brien*

I have two questions about Arnold Schwarzenegger. What does he know, and when will he know it?

—*Bill Maher*

Arnold Schwarzenegger is now governor of California. He is a very shrewd man—he already has all of his sex scandals behind him.
—*David Letterman*

The big political news, Arnold Schwarzenegger announced he's running for governor of California, and already, people are chanting, "four more vowels, four more vowels."
—*Craig Kilborn*

Yesterday, Arnold Schwarzenegger announced he would run for governor of California. The announcement was good news for Florida residents who now live in the second flakiest state in the country.
—*Conan O'Brien*

Arnold Schwarzenegger has announced he will refuse his $175,000 salary and will work for free. I believe he will be worth every penny.
—*Craig Kilborn*

More problems for Governor-elect Arnold Schwarzenegger. California Attorney General Bill Locklear has suggested a special toll free number be set up for women to call in allegations about Arnold's past. I have a better idea—why not make it a 900 number and charge $1.99 a minute. We'll pay off that $33 billion dollars right there.
—*Jay Leno*

California Governor Arnold Schwarzenegger's popularity has been slipping in recent months as residents slowly begin to realize they elected Arnold Schwarzenegger to be their governor.
—*Tina Fey*

In Washington, Arnold Schwarzenegger met with Vice President
Dick Cheney. So, the Terminator met the Defibrillator. The
difference between Schwarzenegger and Cheney is that when
Cheney grabs a chest, it's his own.

—*Jay Leno*

In his first news conference after being elected governor of California,
Arnold Schwarzenegger promised to clean house in Sacramento. He
also threatened to molest the energy crisis, and date rape the deficit.

—*Tina Fey*, Saturday Night Live's "*Weekend Update*"

People here in Los Angeles are disgusted now about a sex scandal
involving Arnold Schwarzenegger. Apparently for seven years, he
carried on a sexual relationship with his own wife.

—*Craig Kilborn*

Time was, our leaders were all veterans of World War II, the Korean conflict or even the struggle for civil rights. But now, with the election of Jesse Ventura in Minnesota and Arnold Schwarzenegger in California, it is clear that the next generation of political leaders will all come from the movie *Predator*.

—*Stephen Colbert*, The Daily Show with Jon Stewart

Arnold Schwarzenegger spoke tonight at the convention. At first they were planning on having Arnold speak on the same night as President Bush but, then they realized, oh no, the convention interpreter's head would have exploded.

—*Jay Leno*

Arnold Schwarzenegger got places by lifting things, heavy things. We, we avoid lifting things at all cost. How bad must have the previous Governor of California been—how much children's blood must he have spilt during his reign?

*—writer Dylan Moran*

New rule: No do-overs. Once you elect an official, unless he runs off with public funds or gets caught with kiddie porn, you're stuck with him. He's the governor, not some dude you married in Las Vegas.

*—Bill Maher*

Seeing Arnold's performance as governor has really changed my mind about actors becoming politicians. I don't know what I'm going to do with my box of "Van Damme in '08" t-shirts.

*—San Francisco comedian John Maclain in reference to B-movie fisticuff actor Jean Claude Van Damme*

# IX

# A GLITTER OF GREEN AND GOLD WONDER

*California's Natural Beauty*

Yosemite Valley, to me, is always a sunrise, a glitter of green and golden wonder in a vast edifice of stone and space.

—*Ansel Adams*

Every thing on shore looked bright and beautiful, the hills covered with grass and flowers, the live-oaks so serene and homelike, and the low adobe houses, with red-tiled roofs and whitened walls, contrasted well with the dark pinetrees behind, making a decidedly good impression upon us who had come so far to spy out the land. Nothing could be more peaceful in its looks than Monterey in January, 1847.

—*General William T. Sherman*

John the Baptist was not more eager to get all of his fellow sinners into the Jordan River than I to baptize all of mine in the beauty of God's mountains.

—*John Muir, 1868*

Were you all with us and our horses fresh it would notwithstanding
all its hardships be to me a perfect pleasure trip. There is so much
variety and excitement about it, and the scenery through which we
are constantly passing is so wild and magnificently grand that it
elevates the soul from earth to heaven and causes such an elasticity
of mind that I forget I am old.

—*settler Harriet Ward, in a letter to her children,* 1848

One thinks of the desert as a barren sandy waste, minus water, trees
and other vegetation, clouds, and all the color and beauty of nature
of more favored districts. Not so. Water is scarce, it is true . . . But
color, beautiful, brilliant, magnificent color, is here any and every
day of the year, and from earliest dawn until the last traces of the
evening sun have faded away, only to give place to moonlight
unsurpassed anywhere in the world. Truly, the desert is far from
being the dry, desolate, uninteresting region it is commonly pictured.

—*Charles Franklin Carter,* Stories of the Old Missions
of California, *"The Indian Sibyl's Prophecy"*

Away in the extreme south, a little hill of fog arose against the sky above the general surface, and as it had already caught the sun, it shone on the horizon like the top-sails of some giant ship. There were huge waves, stationary, as it seemed, like waves in a frozen sea; and yet, as I looked again, I was not sure but they were moving after all, with a slow and august advance. And while I was yet doubting, a promontory of the hills some four or five miles away, conspicuous by a bouquet of tall pines, was in a single instant overtaken and swallowed up.

—*Robert Louis Stevenson, "The Sea Fogs"*

At the pass, Beckwourth dismounted and helped the girl off the horse. An autumn wind had come up, stinging their faces, whipping their clothes. Storm clouds were gathering, darkening all the landscape except the valley lying to the west below them. The sun lighted it as if on purpose for this moment. Jim pointed to the glowing valley lying against a range of blue. "There, little girl," he said, "there is California! There is your kingdom!"

—*Janice Albert, "Ina Coolbrith and the California Frontier"*

The Valley is full of sun but glorious Sierras are piled above the South Dome and Staff King. I mean the bossy cumuli that are daily upheaved at this season, making a cloud period yet grander than the rock-sculpturing, Yosemite making, forest-planting glacial period. Yesterday we had our first midday shower; the pines waved gloriously at its approach, the woodpeckers beat about as if alarmed, but the humming-bird moths thought the cloud shadows belonged to evening and came down to eat among the mints. All the firs and rocks of Starr King were bathily dripped before the Valley was vouchsafed a single drop. After the splendid blessing the afternoon was veiled in calm clouds, and one of intensely beautiful pattern and gorgeously irised was stationed over Eagle Rock at the sunset.

—*John Muir*

The few scientific men who have written upon this region tell us that Yosemite Valley is unlike anything else, an exceptional creation, separate in all respects from all other valleys, but such is not true. Yosemite is one of many, one chapter of a great mountain book written by the same pen of ice which the Lord long ago passed over every page of our great Sierra Nevadas. I know how Yosemite and all the other valleys of these magnificent mountains were made and the next year or two of my life will be occupied chiefly in writing their history in a human book—a glorious subject, which God help me preach aright.

*—John Muir*

It was a Thursday, and it was one of those days in Monterey when the air is washed and polished like a lens, so that you can see the houses in Santa Cruz twenty miles across the bay and you can see the redwood trees on a mountain above Watsonville.

*—John Steinbeck,* Sweet Thursday

In many spots sand drifts like snow. In these areas—called blowouts—sand breaks loose of the vegetation stabilizing it and flows freely, driven east by the prevailing winds off the ocean. The sand blows until a plant, usually a burweed, takes root. Drifting sand gathers in the lee of its brances, forcing the bush to grow higher to stay clear of the latest accumulation. More plants, such as primrose and lupine, sprout around the burweed, and their roots further secure the hillside. Eventually a new hillock is formed.

—*David Wicinas*, Sagebrush and Cappuccinos: Confessions of an L.A. Naturalist

It is enough occupation, when no storm is brewing, to watch the cloud currents and the chambers of the sky. From Kearsarge, say, you look over Inyo and find pink soft cloud masses asleep on the level desert air; south of you hurries a white troop late to some gathering of their kind at the back of Oppapago; nosing the foot of Waban, a woolly mist creeps south. In the clean, smooth paths of the middle sky and highest up in air, drift, unshepherded, small flocks ranging contrarily.

—*Mary Austin*, Land of Little Rain

The edges of the trees burned with a pale violet light and their centers gradually turned from deep purple to black. The same violet piping, like a Neon tube, outlined the tops of the ugly, hump-backed hills and they were almost beautiful.

—*Nathaniel West*, The Day of the Locust

We remember once standing in Cucamonga in a perfectly clear atmosphere, while to the south was a stream of sand, like an immense river, carried in the windstorm . . . It looked as if one could step into it and out, as into and out of a stream of water. Like a swift current of water, the sand stream is parted by elevations, leaving these as islands peering above the sand cloud.

—The Philosophy of Sandstorms, 1880

For it is a land of illusion, a place in the mind, a shimmering mirage of riches and mystery and death. These illusions have distorted its landscape and contorted its history.

> —*journalist Richard Lingenfelter on Death Valley*

⌣‾

Yearly the spring fret floats the loose population of Jimville out into the desolate waste hot lands, guiding by the peaks and a few rarely touched water-holes, always, always with the golden hope. They develop prospects and grow rich, develop others and grow poor but never embittered. Say the hills, It is all one, there is gold enough, time enough, and men enough to come after you. And at Jimville they understand the language of the hills.

> —*Mary Austin*, Jimville—A Bret Harte Town

⌣‾

Yosemite Park is a place of rest, a refuge from the roar and dust and weary, nervous, wasting work of the lowlands, in which one gains the advantages of both solitude and society. Nowhere will you find more company of a soothing peace-be-still kind. Your animal fellow-beings, so seldom regarded in civilization, and every rock-brow and mountain, stream, and lake, and every plant soon come to be regarded as brothers; even one learns to like the storms and clouds and tireless winds.

—*John Muir*

Bear Valley is the hidden treasure of the Sierra.

—*Lloyd Bridges*

Truth comes to us from the past, as gold is washed down from the mountains of Sierra Nevada, in minute but precious particles, and intermixed with infinite alloy, the debris of the centuries.

—*Christian Bovee*

Then it seemed to me that the Sierra should be called, not the
Nevada or Snowy Range, but the Range of Light. And after ten
years of wandering and wondering in the heart of it, rejoicing in its
glorious floods of light, the white beams of the morning streaming
through the passes, the noonday radiance on the crystal rocks, the
flush of the alpenglow, and the irised spray of countless waterfalls,
it still seems above all others the Range of Light.

—*John Muir*

Instead, I could enjoy a simpler, more elemental existence:
watching the rising sun blaze across the [Topanga] sandstone
palisades, scraping bicepts and deltoids and quadriceps on harsh,
unyielding rock; tiptoeing through the valley's remotest glans;
hearing the whisper of its streams; crushing sagebrush leaves in
my hand and smelling their pungence.

—*David Wicinas*, Sagebrush and Cappuccinos:
Confessions of an L.A. Naturalist

[The missionaries] inspected the terrain and found an extensive and attractive plain . . . adjoining a river, which they named the San Antonio. To them it seemed quite an apt site for the new mission because of the good current of water flowing even in the month of July, which is the high point of the dry season. They realized that they could readily utilize the river for irrigation purposes. They all concurred in the choice of this spot for the settlement; whereupon the Venerable Father [Serra] ordered the mules to be unloaded and the bells hung from the branch of a tree.

—*Francisco Palóu, a companion of Father Junipero Serra,* 1787

Growing up in northern California has had a big influence on my love and respect for the outdoors. When I lived in Oakland, we would think nothing of driving to Half Moon Bay and Santa Cruz one day and then driving to the foothills of the Sierras the next day.

—*Tom Hanks*

An afternoon drive from Los Angeles will take you up into the high mountains, where eagles circle above the forests and the cold blue lakes, or out over the Mojave Desert, with its weird vegetation and immense vistas. Not very far away are Death Valley, and Yosemite, and Sequoia Forest with its giant trees which were growing long before the Parthenon was built; they are the oldest living things in the world. One should visit such places often, and be conscious, in the midst of the city, of their surrounding presence. For this is the real nature of California and the secret of its fascination; this untamed, undomesticated, aloof, prehistoric landscape which relentlessly reminds the traveller of his human condition and the circumstances of his tenure upon the earth.

—*Christopher Isherwood*

In California in the early Spring,
There are pale yellow mornings, when the mist burns slowly into day,
The air stings like Autumn, clarifies the pain—
Well, I have dreamed this coast myself.

—*poet Robert Hass*

The first treasure California began to surrender after the Gold Rush was the oldest: her land.

*—author John Jakes*

All scenery in California requires distance to it its highest charm.

*—Mark Twain*

The California climate is perfect for bikes [motorcycles], as well as surfboards, convertibles, swimming pools and abulia.

*—H. S. Thompson,* Hell's Angels

Another glorious day, the air as delicious to the lungs as nectar to the tongue.

*—John Muir,* My First Summer in the Sierra

After about an hour I passed over into California [from Nevada], into a shimmering landscape of bleached earth and patchy creosote bushes called the Devil's Playground. The sunlight glared. The far-off Soda Mountains quivered and distant cars coming towards me looked like balls of fire . . .

*—Bill Bryson, driving through Death Valley, from* The Lost Continent

Three miles from Truckee, Nevada County California, lies one of the fairest and most picturesque lakes in all the Sierra [Donner Lake]. Above, and on either side, are lofty mountains with casteliated granite crests, while below, at the mouth of the lake, a grassy meadow valley widens out and extends to almost Truckee.

—C. F. McGlashan, History of the Donner Party, *describing the site of the ill-fated Donner Party, some of whom resorted to cannibalism while snowbound in the mountains*

Inland rises the great Sierra, with spreading ridge and foothill, like some huge, sprawling centipede, its granite back unbroken for a thousand miles. Frost-torn peaks, of every height and bearing, pierce the blue wastes above. Their slopes are dark with forests of sugar pines and giant sequoias, the mightiest of trees, in whose silent aisles one may wander all day long and see no sign of man.

—David Starr Jordan, first president of Stanford University, *from* California and Californians, *1907*

The sides of the canyon were clothed and garlanded in various
shades of green from top to bottom. Black oak trees in their fresh,
new garbs of early summer, intermingled with stately pines. All
space between these trees was filled with a rich growth of all the
flowering shrubs known to our California mountains.

—*J. A. Graves*, Out of Doors:
California and Oregon, *1912*

At San Quentin [prison and island] nature is at her best, and man
at his worst.

—*Bishop O.P. Fitzgerald*,
California Sketches, *1860*

A few minutes ago every tree was excited, bowing to the roaring storm, waving, swirling, tossing their branches in glorious enthusiasm like worship. But though to the outer ear these trees are now silent, their songs never cease.

—*John Muir*

The Sanramoon Valley is one of the most productive spots in the whole State [of California] and is under fine cultivation. Fields of wheat were standing fence high, green as a meadow, and level as a house floor, and so heavily laden as to tremble in the breeze from their weight.

—*Caroline M. Churchill*, Over the Purple Hills, *1881*

Take the State [of California] over, the scenery is grandly magnificent and beautiful beyond description; but the contemplating emigrant must bear in mind the fact, that scenery is mighty poor feed for a hungry family; baked beans as a steady diet, will beat scenery two to one. This is partly the Author's opinion.
                    —*W. S. Walker,* Glimpses of Hungryland, 1880

Our seaside life is at its glory when the children from Los Angeles seek its summer shores at the times of the lower-low tides. There are the marine treasures to be found . . . There is a fascination in walking, riding, or driving along the untrodden sands of a stretch of beach. What may not one expect to find just around that curve in the shore, just beyond those rocks? Some curiosity, or feathery sea-fern more beautiful than any in your basket, some pebble brighter than Redondo's brightest, were that possible.
                    —*Frederick Hastings Rindge,*
        Happy Days in Southern California, 1898

The prevailing sunlight of California is indeed a pleasant thing. It fills every nerve and sense with the heat and the strength, the glory and the excellency of life.

—*Walter M. Fisher*, The Californians, 1876

You could, if you wished, fry an egg on the roof your car in Death Valley, then drive thirty miles into the [Sierra Nevada] mountains and quick-freeze it in a snowbank.

—*Bill Bryson*, The Lost Continent

# X

# THE BIG BURRITO

*California in Politics*

You won't have Nixon to kick around anymore. Because gentlemen, this is my last press conference.
—*Richard Nixon in 1962 after losing the race for Governor of California*

⁓

There was no way he could save himself. It was like a Greek tragedy.
—*attributed to reporter Helen Thomas in reference to Richard Nixon*

⁓

I love California; I practically grew up in Phoenix.
—*Dan Quayle*

⁓

Sandlotter, n. A vertebrate mammal holding the political views of
Denis Kearney, a notorious demagogue of San Francisco, whose
audiences gathered in the open spaces (sandlots) of the town. True
to the traditions of his species, this leader of the proletariat was
finally bought off by his law-and-order enemies, living prosperously
silent and dying impenitently rich. But before his treason he
imposed upon California a constitution that was a confection of sin
in a diction of solecisms. The similarity between the words sandlotter
and sansculotte is problematically significant, but indubitably
suggestive.

> —*Ambrose Bierce,* The Devil's Dictionary

We need Hawaii just as much and a good deal more than we did
California. It is Manifest Destiny.

> —*President William McKinley*

Whatever starts in California unfortunately has a tendency
to spread.

> —*Jimmy Carter, a remark in a cabinet meeting in 1977*

My fellow Americans, this is an amazing moment for me. To think
that a once scrawny boy from Austria could grow up to become
Governor of California and stand in Madison Square Garden to
speak on behalf of the President of the United States, that is an
immigrant's dream. It is the American dream.

> —*Arnold Schwarzenegger*

I have left specific instructions that I do not want to be brought
back during a Republican administration.

> —*Timothy Leary, although his remains were*
> *cremated and then launched into space*

California has become the first American state where there is no majority race, and we're doing just fine. If you look around the room, you can see a microcosm of what we can do in the world. . . . You should be hopeful on balance about the future. But it's like any future since the beginning of time—you're going to have to make it.
—*President Bill Clinton*

So when you go up against the Far Right you go up against the big financial special interests like the Halliburtons of the world, the big oil companies, the big energy companies who work so hard to rip us off.
—*Barbara Boxer, junior senator from California*

There is a refreshing note to all of this.
—*Jerry Brown, former governor of California, reflecting on the recall election of Gray Davis*

Most analysts would agree that if all the undocumented immigrants in California were deported in one day, our state would experience a severe economic downturn. This does not even consider the many cultural and spiritual gifts theses immigrants bring to our state and nation.

—*clergyman Roger Mahony*

When we finally have this recall election in October, there could be as many as 200 people on the ballot. And you know what's really scary? Most of them don't know the first thing about driving a state into bankruptcy. They're no experts like Governor Gray Davis.

—*Jay Leno*

California is choosing between the lesser of, uh, 300 evils.

—*Jon Stewart*

Larry Flynt, running for the governor of California. His goal—
changing our state bird to the spread eagle.

—*Craig Kilborn*

I'd been under contract to Warner Brothers for a number of years—
when [studio head Jack Warner] heard I was running for governor
[of California]. I understand that he said, "No, no. Jimmy Stewart
for governor. Reagan for best friend."

—*Ronald Reagan*

Women are the engine driving the growth in California's economy.
Women make California's economy unique.

—*Arnold Schwarzenegger*

There is no better place to be a woman with hopes and dreams than California. The jobs are better paying and more fulfilling and California is a much better place because of that.

—*Arnold Schwarzenegger*

It's disgusting even if this amounts to applying the standards of the twenty-first century to events of the mid-1970s. Schwarzenegger isn't running for governor of California in 1975.

—*journalist Michael Kinsley*

It's California I'm worried about. I don't want you to become a laughingstock, a carnival or the beginning of a circus in America where we just throw people out as soon as they make a tough decision. . . . Don't do this. Don't do this.

—*President Bill Clinton*

I know there's a great deal that Arnold Schwarzenegger could teach me about making movies. There's a great deal I could teach him about the fiscal reforms that are needed—desperately needed—to set California back in good order.

*—politician Tom McClintock*

I would rather be governor of California than own Austria.

*—Arnold Schwarzenegger*

Politics is supposed to be the second oldest profession. I have come to realize that it bears a very close resemblance to the first.

*—Ronald Reagan*

To say that people would cease to come to California if they would have to pay more taxes is to underestimate the advantages of being in California—mightily.

—*Warren Beatty*

There's no question that California, in the last three or four years, has been privileged to add disproportionately to the economic growth of America, and to contribute to its technological productivity.

—*Gray Davis, former governor of California*

Protect the Earth, Serve the People and Explore the Universe.

—*Jerry Brown campaign slogan in the 1980 presidential primary*

That man [Jerry Brown] is like 500 pounds of Jello.
                    —*Willie Brown, former Mayor of San Francisco*

I am Governor Jerry Brown
My aura smiles
And never frowns
Soon I will be president . . .
                    —*from the song "California Uber Alles,"*
                    *by San Francisco punk band The Dead Kennedys*

My political ideal is my home town in Vermont, with more sex.
                    —*John H. Schaar, Professor Emeritus of Political*
                    *Philosophy at the University of California at Santa Cruz*

Why should we put a plan out? Our plan is to stop him [G. W. Bush]. He must be stopped.

*—Speaker of the House Nancy Pelosi*

I pledged California to a Northern Republic and to a flag that should have no treacherous threads of cotton in its warp, and the audience came down in thunder.

*—Thomas Starr King, clergyman*

They say California's the big burrito; Texas is a big taco right now. We want to follow that through. Florida is a big tamale.

*—Dan Rather, former CBS anchorman*

And so today I am calling upon both sides in the red-blue rift to reach out. Maybe we could have a cultural-exchange program between red and blue states. For example, a delegation from Texas could go to California and show the Californians how to do some traditional Texas thing such as castrate a bull using only your teeth, and then the Californians could show the Texans how to rearrange their football stadiums in accordance with the principles of "feng shui" (for openers, both goalposts should be at the west end of the field).

—*Dave Barry*

While campaigning for U.S. Senator from California in 1964, I made love practically every night with the wife of a famous actor.

—*Pierre Salinger, politician*

I'm not worried about the deficit. It is big enough to take care of itself.

—*Ronald Reagan, joke at the Gridiron Club, 1984*

I toured California in the interests of the Peace Corps, but if I were to do that in Illinois, people would take me for a candidate, as I'm not.

—*Sargent Shriver, politician*

When we acquired California and New Mexico this party, scorning all compromises and all concessions, demanded that slavery should be forever excluded from them, and all other acquisitions of the Republic, either by purchase or conquest, forever.

—*Robert Toombs, politician*

I was raised in the West. The West of Texas. It's pretty close to California. In more ways than Washington, D.C., is close to California.

—*George H. Bush*

Legislators represent people, not trees or acres. Legislators are elected by voters, not farms or cities or economic interests.

> —*attributed to Earl Warren, 30th governor of California,*
> *14th chief justice of the United States*

I have left orders to be awakened at any time in case of national emergency, even if I'm in a cabinet meeting.

> —*Ronald Reagan, repeated often during his presidency*

The difference between a democracy and a dictatorship is that in a democracy you vote first and take orders later; in a dictatorship you don't have to waste your time voting.

> —*Los Angeles poet Charles Bukowski,*
> *often mistakenly associated with the Beat Generation*

[Freedom of speech] is the thing that marks us just below the angels.

—*Mario Savio, leader of the Free Speech Movement at Berkeley in the 1960s*

The California crunch really is the result of not enough power-generating plants and then not enough power to power the power of generating plants.

—*George W. Bush, interview with the* New York Times, *Jan. 14, 2001*

Ralph Nader chose the man with whom to share the responsibility of running a distant third, California activist Peter Camejo. You may remember that Camejo ran for president in 1976 on the Socialist Workers Party ticket. Actually, you might only remember that if you run a lesbian vegetarian bookstore.

—*Jon Stewart*

Maybe it will take a woman to clean up the House.

> —*Speaker of the House Nancy Pelosi,*
> *in an interview with Barbara Walters*

Being desirous of allaying the dissensions of party strife now existing within our realm, I do hereby dissolve and abolish the Democratic and Republican parties . . .

> —*Joshua Abraham Norton, Emperor Norton I, beloved*
> *and eccentric nineteenth-century resident of San Francisco*
> *who proclaimed himself Emperor of the United States*
> *and Protector of Mexico*

# XI

# TOTALLY RAD

*Native Californians Speak*

Start slow . . . and taper off.
                    —*renowned and beloved Bay Area runner Walt Stack*

I was right then, I'm right now. I think time has proven me right.
                    —*Republican politician Pete Wilson*

A little vagueness goes a long way in this business.
                    —*Jerry Brown, former governor of California*

The clearest way into the Universe is through a forest wilderness.
                    —*John Muir*, John of the Mountains

Why not? The ball isn't very heavy. And besides, he doesn't belong to a union.

  *—John H. McKay, former head coach of the USC Trojans football team, on why his tailbacks carried the ball so much*

I may go down in history as the guy who killed Pluto.

  *—Michael E. Brown, professor of planetary astronomy at the California Institute of Technology, who lobbied and succeeded in having Pluto declassified as a planet*

Epidemiology is like a bikini: what is revealed is interesting; what is concealed is crucial.

  *—Peter Duesberg, award-winning professor of molecular and cell biology at the University of California, Berkely*

The future is not some place we are going to, but one we are creating. The paths are not to be found, but made, and the activity of making them, changes both the maker and the destination.
—*John H. Schaar, Professor Emeritus of Political Philosophy at the University of California at Santa Cruz*

It was so gnarly, dude, and I'd been on his show a couple times, so I basically figured we were homies. I yelled over to him, and I was like, "Yo, Reg, what up?" And then get this: He called me the Red Onion! Dude, it was so epic. It was totally rad.
—*Shaun White, Olympic-gold winning snowboarder based in Carlsbad, California, on sitting next to Regis Philbin at a Knicks game*

If "no" meant "no" then every man would die a virgin.
—*Daniel Tosh, L.A. comedian*

Before I pay for it, I pray for it.
—*Rick Warren, Evangelical Christian pastor from San José*

A fundamentalist is someone who hates sin more than he loves virtue.
—*John H. Schaar, Professor Emeritus of Political Philosophy
at the University of California at Santa Cruz*

I'm not a woman. I'm a force of nature.
—*San Francisco's Courtney Love*

You can't trust anybody over thirty.
—*Jack Weinberg, member of Berkeley
Free Speech Movement in the 1960s*

Kissing—and I mean like, yummy, smacking kissing—is the most delicious, most beautiful and passionate thing that two people can do, bar none. Better than sex, hands down.

*—attributed to actress Drew Barrymore*

I'll never be hung in effigy. Before every season I send my men out to buy up all the rope in Los Angeles.

*—John H. MacKay, former head coach of the USC Trojans football team*

You can't disobey the rules every time you disapprove. However, when you're considering something that constitutes an extreme abridgement of your rights, conscience is the court of last resort.

*—Mario Savio, leader of the Free Speech Movement at Berkeley in the 1960s*

THE BEARS HAVE WON!!! THE BEARS HAVE WON!!! Oh my god! The most amazing sensational, dramatic, heart rending . . . exciting, thrilling finish in the history of college football. California has won the Big Game over Stanford!

> —*words of Cal radio announcer Joe Starkey,*
> *when in 1982 Cal used five laterals on the last*
> *play of the game to beat Stanford 25-20*

I don't think that a touchdown can be scored when you've got a whole band on the field. Now if he runs through three trombone guys, a tuba player, and two drum players, and dodges . . . and then runs right over a trombone player at the goal line and they call it a touchdown then, yeah, I think that that probably shouldn't have been called.

> —*John Elway, former Denver Broncos Pro-Bowl*
> *quarterback and Stanford signal caller*
> *on losing to Cal 25-20*

This one summer I was hired by this rich dude to check out an island for him. It was nice and tropical, but it was full of dinosaurs. Then the power went out and all these dinosaurs broke out of their cages. They were eating and killing everyone, causing a whole bunch of trouble, so I took off. That guy still owes me some money.
  —*Shaun White, Olympic-gold winning snowboarder based in Carlsbad, California, when asked what his worst summer job was*

What was most significant about the lunar voyage was not that men set foot on the moon but that they set eye on the Earth.
  —*Norman Cousins, former Adjunct Professor of Medical Humanities at the University of California*

I don't suffer from insanity, I enjoy every minute of it.
  —*Los Angeles-born actress Angelina Jolie*

Only by going alone in silence, without baggage, can one truly get into the heart of the wilderness. All other travel is mere dust and hotels and baggage and chatter.

—*John Muir, letter to his wife "Louie,"*
*from* Life and Letters of John Muir

I always turn to the sports pages first. The sports page records people's accomplishments; the front page nothing but man's failures.

—*attributed to Earl Warren, 30th governor of California,*
*14th chief justice of the United States*

I'm all for women who get plastic surgery. Because plastic surgery allows you to make your outer appearance resemble your inner appearance—fake.

—*L.A. comedian Daniel Tosh*

We, the undersigned, gathered in Pilgrimage to the capital of the State in Sacramento in penance for all the failings of Farm Workers as free and sovereign men, do solemnly declare before the civilized world which judges our actions, and before the nation to which we belong, the propositions we have formulated to end the injustice that oppresses us.

*—activist César Chávez, from The Plan of Delano, 1965*

Sock it to me?

*—Richard Nixon on* Laugh-In

I believe that if you didn't see my picture in magazines, I would just be another California girl sitting at a café or walking along the beach.

*—actress Cameron Diaz*

You're only as young as the last time you changed your mind.

> —*Timothy Leary*

I hope we find a cure for every major disease. I'm tired of walking 5k.

> —*Daniel Tosh, L.A. comedian*

Bite my ass, Krispy Kreme!

> —*Julia Roberts as the reluctant*
> *environmental crusader Erin Brockovich*

I think I've been able to fool a lot of people because I know I'm a dork. I'm a geek.

> —*Gwen Stefani, Anaheim native and rock star*

I don't like the Girl Scouts. I can't trust an adolescent female
paramilitary organization that sells highly addictive baked goods.
*—John Maclain, San Francisco comedian*

My fellow Americans, I'm pleased to tell you today that I've signed
legislation that will outlaw Russia forever. We begin bombing in
five minutes.
*—Ronald Reagan during a microphone check in
1984, unaware he was being broadcast*

Don't wanna be an American idiot
Don't wanna nation under the new media
*—"American Idiot," lyrics by California's
seminal pop-punk band Green Day*

My ambition is handicapped by my laziness.
  —*Los Angeles poet Charles Bukowski, often mistakenly*
  *associated with the Beat Generation*

I'm the Chosen One, and I choose to be shopping.
  —*Sarah Michelle Gellar as Buffy, the Vampire Slayer*

It's ironic that those who till the soil, cultivate and harvest fruits and vegetables and other foods that fill your tables with abundance have nothing left for themselves.
  —*activist, César Chávez*

All I need are some tasty waves, a cool buzz, and I'm fine.
   —*Sean Penn as Jeff Spicoli,* Fast Times at Ridgemont High

The girl with the junk in the trunk will bunk with the best hunk.
   —*Amy Lee, lead singer, lyricist of the band Evanescence*

As a youngster growing up, I had the unenviable experience of digesting the most negative stereotypes about Black folks being illiterate, being criminals, being violent, being promiscuous, being indolent, etc. When you're spoon-fed these things on an incessant basis, you eventually morph into those negative stereotypes, unwittingly. That's what happened to me. I became the stereotypes that I was spoon-fed.
   —*Stanley "Tookie" Williams, early leader of the Crips street gang from South Central L.A.*

If something comes to life in others because of you, they you have made an approach to immortality.

*—Norman Cousins, former Adjunct Professor of Medical Humanities at the University of California*

⌒

The day someone quits school he is condemning himself to a future of poverty.

*—Jaime Escalante, award-winning educator who got young, poor latinos to pass the AP exam in calculus at Garfield High School in Los Angeles*

⌒

Beware the lollipop of mediocrity; lick it once and you'll suck forever.

*—attributed to Brian Wilson of the Beach Boys*

⌒

[To his students] There will be no free rides, no excuses. You already have two strikes against you: your name and your complexion. Because of these two strikes, there are some people in this world who will assume that you know less than you do. Math is the great equalizer . . . When you go for a job, the person giving you that job will not want to hear your problems; ergo, neither do I. You're going to work harder here than you've ever worked anywhere else. And the only thing I ask from you is ganas. Desire.

—*Edward James Olmos as Jaime Escalante*
*in the film* Stand and Deliver

It started out—my mom and dad took a little vacation to Mexico and they left $250 for food. But instead of food we went and bought some instruments. We got a bass, guitar and a set of drums . . . I was 19. Dennis [Wilson] was 15. Carl [Wilson] was 17. Mike [Love] was 18. Al [Jardine] was 19. And so we wrote a song called "Surfin'" in my living room . . . and that's how it all started.

—*Brian Wilson on the formation of the Beach Boys*

And Sandy Koufax, whose name will always remind you of strikeouts, did it with a flourish. He struck out the last six consecutive batters. So when he wrote his name in capital letters in the record books, that "K" stands out even more than the O-U-F-A-X.
> —*Vin Scully, from the transcription of his play-by-play of the legendary L.A. Dodgers pitcher's no-hit, no-run game of September 9, 1965*

Everyone needs a hug. It changes your metabolism.
> —*Dr. Felice Leonardo Buscaglia, professor at USC*

Don't sweat the petty things and don't pet the sweaty things.
> —*Amy Lee, lead singer, lyricist of the band Evanescence*

To all that come to this happy place: Welcome. Disneyland is your land. Here age relives fond memories of the past, and here youth may savor the challenge and promise of the future. Disneyland is dedicated to the ideals, the dreams, and the hard facts that have created America; with the hope that it will be a source of joy and inspiration to all the world.

*—Walt Disney, from his speech on the opening day of Disneyland (July 17, 1955)*

All I wanna do is graduate from high school, move to Europe, marry Christian Slater, and die. Now, that may not sound too exciting to a scone-head like you, but I think it's swell.

*—Sarah Michelle Gellar as Buffy, the Vampire Slayer*

If you want to know who your friends are, get yourself a jail sentence.
—*Los Angeles poet Charles Bukowski,*
*often mistakenly associated with the Beat Generation*

Drugs are the religion of the twenty-first century.
—*Timothy Leary*

Books should confuse. Literature abhors the typical. Literature flows to the particular, the mundane, the greasiness of paper, the taste of warm beer, the smell of onion or quince.
—*Richard Rodriguez, Mexican-American writer,*
*associate editor with the Pacific News Service,*
*from* Brown: The Last Discovery of America

Great sex for a single man is a lot like playing tennis. It's fun, recreational in nature, makes you sweat, requires a partner of equal ability and the object is to avoid " LOVE" at all costs . . .

*—John Zeigler, L.A. radio talk show host*

I love Mickey Mouse more than any woman I've ever known.

*—Walt Disney*

Aw, get a piece of fat and slide off.

*—Phil Hendrie, comedy talk radio show host*

Learnin' about Cuba. Havin' some food.

*—Sean Penn as Jeff Spicoli,* Fast Times at Ridgemont High

There ain't no such thing as a free lunch.
>—*Walter Morrow*, San Francisco News, *1949*

Everybody has to die, but I always believed an exception would be made in my case. Now what?
>—*William Saroyan, five days before his death*

If you live life right death is a joke as far as fear is concerned
>—*Will Roger's epitaph*

Hindsight is always 20/20.
>—*Billy Wilder*

You don't get rich writing science fiction. If you want to get rich, you start a religion.

—*L. Ron Hubbard, the founder of Scientology*

Say "Dodgers" and people know you're talking about baseball. Say "Braves" and they ask, "What reservation?" Say "Reds" and they think of communism. Say "Padres" and they look around for a priest.

—*Tommy Lasorda, former manager of the L.A. Dodgers*

If we had any nerve at all, if we had any real balls as a society, or whatever you need, whatever quality you need, real character, we would make an effort to really address the wrongs in this society, righteously.

—*Jerry Garcia*

Never trust a computer you can't throw out a window.
*—Steve Wozniak, co-founder of Apple Computers*

You know, I said it once before, a few days ago, that Kirk Gibson
was not the Most Valuable Player; that the Most Valuable Player for
the Dodgers was Tinkerbell. But, tonight, I think Tinkerbell backed
off for Kirk Gibson.
*—Vin Scully after a physically wrecked Gibson hit*
*the homerun that won Game 1 of the 1988 World Series*
*for the L.A. Dodgers against the Oakland A's*

People, I just want to say, you know, can we all get along?
*—Rodney King's plead for peace the third day*
*of the Los Angeles riots*

I am no longer a man of war. I die a man of peace.
> —*Stanley "Tookie" Williams, early leader of the Crips street gang from South Central L.A., executed in 2005*

It's 9:15 on 12/13 and another black king will be taken from the scene.
> —*Snoop Dogg, rapper, on the night of the execution of Stanley "Tookie" Williams*

I write about race in America in hopes of undermining the notion of race in America.
> —*Richard Rodriguez, Mexican-American writer, associate editor with the Pacific News Service, from* Brown: The Last Discovery of America

A man goes to knowledge as he goes to war—wide awake, with fear, with respect, and with absolute assurance. Going to knowledge or going to war in any other manner is a mistake, and whoever makes it will live to regret his steps.

—*Carlos Casteneda,* The Teachings of Don Juan

Men used to get drunk on whiskey, which was pretty bad, but I saw a fellow a day or two ago who was drunk on authority, and it wasn't so much different!

—*Coleman Cox,* Listen to This

People will pay more to be entertained than educated.

—*Johnny Carson*

News is something somebody doesn't want printed; all else is advertising.

—*William Randolph Hearst*

Life in California is a little fresher, a little freer, a good deal richer, in its physical aspects, and for these reasons, more intensely and characteristically American.

—*David Starr Jordan, first president of Stanford University, from California and Californians, 1907*

Most people seem to think legalized gambling is immoral and destructive. I see it as simply a tax on people who are unable to grasp basic math.

—*John Zeigler, L.A. radio talk show host*

It is more fun to be sick in California than to be well anywhere else.
                    —*Inez Hayes Irwin, "The Californiacs"*

Five guys on the court working together can achieve more than five talented individuals who come and go as individuals.
                    —*Kareem Abdul-Jabbar, L.A. Lakers legendary center*

[W]hen I ran by guys, I could almost see the anxiety on their faces . . .
                    —*Marcus Allen, Heisman Trophy-winning running back from USC, who later played for the Oakland Raiders*

In junior high a boy poured water down my shirt and yelled, "Now maybe they'll grow."

—*Pamela Anderson*

Quirky is sexy, like scars or chipped teeth. I also like tattoos— they're rebellious.

—*Jennifer Aniston*

Thus the shriek, the caterwaul, the chainsaw gnarlgnashing, the yowl and the whizz that decapitates may be reheard by the adventurous or emotionally damaged as mellifluous bursts of unarguable affirmation.

—*Lester Bangs, Escondido-born rock critic, on punk music*

Perfectionism is the voice of the oppressor.

*—Anne Lamott, San Francisco writer*

There are three types of baseball players: those who make things happen, those who watch it happen, and those who wondered what happens.

*—Tommy Lasorda*

The Goliath of totalitarianism will be brought down by the David of the microchip.

*—Ronald Reagan*

Don't measure yourself by what you have accomplished, but by what you should have accomplished with your ability.
> —*John Wooden, long-time USC basketball coach*

My formula for success is rise early, work late, and strike oil.
> —*J. Paul Getty*

Well, you know, it's really been, you know, quite a trip for me.
> —*Patty Hearst*

You furnish the pictures and I'll furnish the war.
> —*William Randolph Hearst*

Phil Spector's music is permanent wave!
—*Rodney Bingenheimer, influential DJ at KROQ in L.A.,*
*also served as a double for Davy Jones on*
*the TV series,* The Monkees

You do not merely want to be considered just the best of the best.
You want to be considered the only ones who do what you do.
—*Jerry Garcia*

## HEARD IT IN THE VALLEY

"I totally paused! He so totally said that to her!"

"She was like, 'Oh my gawd you have to see this', but I was like,
'No way, you're kidding!'"

"You expect me to wear that? As if!"

"Haven't you heard that before? Duh, it's like a famous quote!"

"You're, like, so totally out of nail polish? What-EVER!"

"So OK, I was totally like, you know, 'I have no idea' or something!"

"Like, ya know, this book is like wow! Great."

## HEARD IT AT THE BEACH

"That dude went aggro when that kook dropped in on him."
(That surfer got quite angry when an inexperienced rider cut him off.)

"Bru, I was so bleak after that flat spell."
(Buddy, I was very disappointed after the waves went flat.)

"Man, I should have worn my rashie today, I am totally Burnt Reynolds."
(Man, I should have worn a rash guard shirt today, I am completely sunburned.)

"Check him out—he's frosted."
(Check out that guy—he's really cute.)

"Yo brah, that beach bunny was bubbles."
(Hey buddy, that girl on the beach was very cute.)

"Brah, check out that filth cutie."
(Buddy, look at that very, very pretty girl.)

"That drop was so gnarly, you must be packing in the stone zone."
(That wave face was so steep (and consequently dangerous), you must be very confident of your surfing abilities.)

"I'm cashed after that three hour session this morning."
(I'm physically exhausted after surfing for three hours this morning.)

"My bro dialed me in yesterday and we scored a wicked session."
(My buddy called me up yesterday, with the knowledge of where the waves were going to be big, and we had some great surfing.)

"Sun's goin' down. This session about dunzo, Bra."
(Day's almost over. This surfing is about to come to an end, buddy.)